TIMES & SEASONS

Grasping God's

PURPOSES & ACTIVITIES

Bobby Conner

Unless otherwise identified, all Scripture quotations in this publication are from *The Holy Bible, New King James Version.* Copyright © 1979, 1980, 1982 by Thomas Nelson, Inc.

ISBN: 978-0-9801639-2-6   0-9801639-2-7

Printed in the United States of America.

Contents

Introduction

God's plans for these end-time days will result in the entire world discovering that His Son, Christ Jesus is King of Kings and Lord of Lords (1 Timothy 6:15 Revelation 19:16. Scripture states that every knee will bow and ever tongue shall confess that Christ is Lord. The scripture declares that the entire earth will be filled with the knowledge of the glory of God Hab 2:14.

The Kingdom of God is advancing swiftly across the nations countless multitudes are turning to Christ. The Spirit of God is anointing ordinary people to do extraordinary exploits for the glory of God. These are days of destiny filled with wonder and excitement. The awe of God is returning to the people of God, filling the heart of God's people with great expectation.

We stand on the verge of the greatest harvest the world

has ever seen. Never forget the Lord will have His harvest. The Spirit of God is at this point in time harvesting the harvesters. Soon over a billion people will be brought into the Kingdom. Truly as stated in Esther 4:14 we are in the Kingdom for such a time as this. You can know for certain that the kingdom is in you for such a day as this. Be confident you are born for this day don't delay move forward walking in victory taking your place as an overcomer embracing fully the destiny God has planned for you.

Divine Commission

part 1

God is looking thought-out the entire earth searching for the upright in heart to them God will prove Himself strong and sure see 2 Chronicles 16:9. The prophetic trumpets must make a clear call in these extremely crucial days in order to prepare a strong confident leadership 1 Cor. 14:8. This is the time to walk with true goal aim and purpose, not drift about in an endless circle. None desire another forty-year trip around the mountain of misguided human efforts. The good news is that we do not need to wait nor wander any longer in the wilderness, it is time to access the Kingdom of God. Now is the time to move forward establishing the Kingdom of God in power.

The Spirit of God is preparing leadership by releasing upon them the anointing that rested upon the sons of Isaccar they had understanding of the time, and were aware of what the people of God should be accomplishing see 1 Chronicles 12:32.

The kingdom of God will not be established by mere words or abilities of men but by the Spirit of God see 2 Corinthians 4:20. This confidence can only come from true union with Christ. It is abiding in His manifested presence that results in our boldness see Proverbs 28:1. These days call for followers of Christ to stand firm knowing who they are in Christ and Who Christ is in them see Col. 2:9-10. God's word declares that in Christ is the fullness of the Godhead and you are complete in HIM.

The Lord has issued an ultimate command. It is unmistakably clear, as followers of Christ we are to be bold, brave, and extremely courageous. Scripture declares in the book of Joshua:

Now it came about after the death of Moses the servant of the LORD that the LORD spoke to Joshua the son of Nun, Moses' servant, saying, "Moses My servant is dead; now therefore arise, cross this Jordan, you and all this people, to the land which I am giving to them, to the sons of Israel. Every place on which the sole of your foot treads, I have given it to you, just as I spoke to Moses. From the wilderness and this Lebanon, even as far as the great river, the river Euphrates, all the land of the Hittites, and as far as the Great Sea toward the setting of the sun will be your territory. No man will be able to stand before you all the days of your life. Just as I have been with Moses, I will be with you; I will not fail you or forsake you.

Be strong and courageous, for you shall give this people possession of the land which I swore to their fathers to give them. Only be strong and very courageous; be careful to do according to all the law which Moses My servant commanded you; do not turn from it to the right or to the left, so that you may have success wherever you go.

This book of the law shall not depart from your mouth, but you shall meditate on it day and night, so that you may be careful to do according to all that

is written in it; for then you will make your way
prosperous, and then you will have success. Have I not
commanded you? Be strong and courageous! Do not
tremble or be dismayed, for the LORD your God is
with you wherever you go."

—Joshua 1:1–9, NASB

The last phrase contains an overwhelming promise; the abiding presence of God. Keep this promise in the mist of your heart: ". . . for the LORD your God is with you wherever you go!" This promise is repeated throughout Scripture and is the foundation of the promise in 1 John 4:4, KJV: "Greater is He [God] that is in you, than he that is in the world." Our God is truly an awesome God! Prepare to behold Him in a manner not seen in our lifetime. God is at this time responding to the invitation of Isaiah 64:1 "Rend the heavens and come down." As an athlete I never liked scrimmage or warm-up I wanted to bell to ring or the whistle to blow and get the real contest underway. The time has come for the true conquest the question is are you ready?

The Conquest

The conquest—the act of conquering—has commenced. This is neither warm-up nor scrimmage; this is the real thing. It is not time to hold back. *Now* is the time to give your all to the Kingdom of God. It is time to arise and advance.

With a spirit of excellence, you must be giving everything for the sake of advancing the cause of Jesus Christ. True Christianity is more about what we do than what we say (1 Corinthians 4:20). It time for action not just mere words.

Not only has Almighty God called you and I to be brave and courageous, He has commissioned us for these important days. We need to be prepared for conquest that brings about a swift and sure change. God's plan for His people is the plan of victory, not defeat (Jeremiah 29:11). We are called and commissioned to be overcomers.

Deep within the soul of every true Christian beats the heart of an overcomer. The word "overcomer" suggests winning after a hard struggle. We are to be strong, willing warriors. Never forget we are fighting from victory not for victory, Christ has won the victory we just move into what He has provided.

Now is the time for the troops of the Lord to volunteer willingly (Psalm 110:3). We are to become history makers and world changers. God has determined the exact time of our birth. Truly we are in the Kingdom for such a time as this (Esther 4:14). Never forget: the Kingdom is in you for such a time as this. Think about it. You had absolutely nothing to do with the timing of your birth. It's God's plan. Looking forward to this day, He determined that you would be a great tool in His hands to fashion the Kingdom of God.

God has confidence in you. It is He working in you, both to will and to do His good pleasure (Philippians 2:13). We discover in Luke 12:32 the Father's good pleasure is to give us the power of His Kingdom. These are decisive days of destiny. God is calling each of us to arise and take our stand for righteousness.

You are extremely unique. Over six billion people are alive on planet Earth, and guess what? Not a single person is like you. That is truly unique.

THE SECRET TO TRUE BOLDNESS

An extremely wise man penned these thought-provoking words:

> *The wicked flee when no one pursues,*
> *But the righteous are bold as a lion.*
>
> —PROVERBS 28:1

Within this short but inspired phrase, we discover an exceptionally significant key: the righteous are bold as a lion. This key is an awesome asset, providing much-needed insight that will unlock the mystery of our weakness. Our lack of demonstrated power is a testimony to our carnality. We must walk in purity if we are to walk in real power.

As we discover the foremost reason for our lack of genuine power—which comes from a lack of genuine holiness—we can move forward with a repentant heart, seeking the Lord to extract from us everything that separates us from Him. Without question, our sin is the principal reason for our continual failure.

God's warning is exceedingly clear: "Make every effort to live in peace with all men and to be holy; without holiness no one will see the Lord" (Hebrews 12:14, NIV). Don't confuse holiness with man-made legalism. True holiness produces overflowing life and peace, while religious legalism produces only barrenness and death. Remember, where the Spirit of the Lord is, there is liberty (2 Corinthians 3:17).

FLESH VERSUS SPIRIT

The Body of Christ must discover and distinguish the immense difference between human arrogance and genuine Holy Spirit boldness; between being driven by our own ambitions and being moved and motivated by God's Spirit. If we continue to act upon our flesh-driven presumptions, failure is assured.

*There is a way that seems right to a man, but in the
end it leads to death.*

—PROVERBS 14:12, NIV

Arrogance is fostered by our flesh—a person's own abilities and human agenda. True boldness, however, is released from an encounter with the Holy Spirit. Scripture paints a picture for us: the righteous shall be as bold as a lion.

Before Simon Peter's dynamitic encounter with the Spirit of God on the day of Pentecost, he wilted under the accusations of a young servant girl. Without the power of God's enabling grace, Peter denied the Lord three times. Yet once he was filled with the Holy Spirit's power and boldness, we see a tremendous transformation in Peter's life. Standing in true authority, he preached one of the fieriest messages in Scripture (Acts 2:16).

A wicked religious spirit will always manifest itself by attempting to counterfeit the original. If this evil spirit cannot get someone moving in pseudo self-confidence, it will cause the person to become weak and timid. It is high time we recognize the difference between timidity and humility, confidence and presumption.

BATTLING BEWITCHMENT

A cunning bewitchment is taking place within the Body of Christ. Paul warned against this spirit when he wrote to the Galatians. This bewitching manifests by using human effort resulting in people attempting to fulfill in the flesh what was begun by the Spirit of God (Galatians 3:1–5).

It's time to ask ourselves some difficult questions such as: Are we being commissioned by God's Spirit or have we birthed our own plans? The distinction can be recognized by failure or success. When one is sent by the Lord, God goes before the person to make a way. However if the person runs without being sent by God, the person is doomed to shame and failure. We must join with Moses: "O Lord if your Presence does not go with us please don't let us take a single step" (Exodus 33:15).

Jesus is the perfect example of being sent by God. Jesus said, "I only do what I see my Father doing; I only say what I hear My Father saying." It was the joy of His heart to do the Father's will. Jesus' life of absolute obedience to the Father's will must become our quest as well. It is the perfect syncopation: we should seek the harmonizing of God's will and our walk. This divine rhythm was reflected in Paul's life when he said: "for me to live is Christ . . ." (Philippians 1:21). Near the end of his journey, he added: "I have fought the good fight. I have finished the course. I have kept the faith" (2 Timothy 4:7, NASB).

How you start is very important, but how we finish is *most* important. The legacy we leave behind is a testimony to how effective we have lived our lives for the purpose of God's Kingdom.

As we read this book, ask yourself: Are you running in your own human zeal, or are you being carried by God's power and might? Remember it's not by human effort, but by His Spirit (Zechariah 4:6). Have you become guilty of walking in the light of your own fire (Isaiah 50:11)?

If so, it's but a dim comparison to the blazing light of the Spirit of Truth. Is it any wonder that you are stumbling about in darkness? While on earth, Jesus told cold, legalistic religious leaders that they were blind leading the blind; both the leaders and their followers were destined to fall into a ditch.

Are you content to drink from your own hand-dug cisterns and forsake the fountain of living water (Jeremiah 2:13)? What a terrible exchange to settle for stale, stagnant, and polluted water instead of the refreshing fountains flowing from the Holy Spirit.

As never before we must walk in the light of God's Word; there, we will find true light for our darkened path (Psalm 119:105, 130). It is only in His light that we can see light (Psalm 36:9).

Scripture reveals to us this precious promise: "For thou wilt light my candle: the LORD my God will enlighten my darkness" (Psalm 18:28, KJV). He alone is the Source of true enlightenment.

The revelation of Christ the King and His Kingdom will become clearer and more concise as we set our hearts to become intimate with Him. Going ever deeper into the ways of the Spirit, we will grow in our knowledge of Christ and His Kingdom. Deep is calling unto the deep; God has been releasing a desire to go higher and deeper than we have ever been. It is to those who present themselves as true friends that Christ will reveal secrets see John 15:15.

Purity Produces Power and Boldness

Let these words resound in your spirit: "the righteous are bold as a lion . . ." (Proverbs 28:1). Asking the Holy Spirit to reveal its meaning. Our heart's desire is that God's Spirit will launch us further into a consuming passion to walk with greater purity; such fervor will result in real Holy Spirit-produced power. This alone is the *key* to walking in sustained supernatural power.

A People of Extreme Burning Passion

In these days the Spirit of Truth will open our eyes to behold deeper truths hidden in Scripture (Matthew 13:16–17). These divine truths will inflame our hearts, igniting within us an extreme burning passion for God's glory and for the advancing of His Kingdom.

God's Spirit is helping us to come to grips with the vast difference between human arrogance and Holy Spirit boldness. Spiritual boldness does not describe many in the Church today. We have grown too accustomed to slick self-promotion, a Madison Avenue-type leadership who advances their own personal agendas. Without a doubt, this is one reason we are walking in so little Holy Spirit-power.

Our heart's cry must be as King David's: "Create in me a clean heart, O God; and renew a right spirit within me" (Psalm 51:9–10, KJV). May our hearts echo this passage:

> *Let Your work appear to Your servants,*
> *And Your glory to their children.*

And let the beauty of the LORD our God be upon us,
And establish the work of our hands for us;
Yes, establish the work of our hands.

—Psalm 90:16–17

We desire to see the works of God, not the plans and purposes of man. Oh, Lord hear or cry and display your might deeds. Only your work will establish the efforts of our hands.

Purity Leads to Power

Holiness is not optional; instead it is essential to the Lord's abiding and powerful presence in our life (Hebrews 12:14). The Lord is looking for a people He can promote, show Himself strong, and fully support everything they put their hand to do (2 Chronicles 16:9).

As I mentioned earlier, Joshua reminded God's people continually to be bold, brave, and courageous. When I questioned the Lord, "Why do you have to keep on reminding us to be bold?" He answered, "Because you're

not!" Our timidity is related to the fact that we are living impurely. With purity comes the Lord's presence. And
where His anointing rests, there will be divine power. In
the life of Jesus, we can see that God's Kingdom was revealed in power, not merely in words (Luke 10:19).

As Christians we are challenged and commanded to be
bold, brave, and courageous in our stand for Christ Jesus.
We are instructed to boldly contend for the faith (Jude
3). If we are not daily contending and defending our faith,
then we are merely pretenders going through the motion.
If our walk does not back up our talk, then we are speaking
hollow, lifeless words. In fact, we are an embarrassment to
the Body of Christ.

But if we are walking in the light of God's Word, we
will have a divine confidence. This boldness comes when
we are walking in integrity and purity of heart. Anointing,
without moral and righteous character, will always result
in shame. The Spirit of God is forging our character; He's
not just releasing gifting.

Scripture tells us that the Kingdom of Heaven suffers violence and the violent take it (the Kingdom) by force. We are not speaking about violence with guns and knives, but rather the true weapons of warfare—fasting, prayer, and holy living. Paul stated that the weapons of our warfare are mighty through God to the pulling down of strongholds (2 Corinthians 10:4–6).

God's ultimate goal is our possessing and manifesting true Christlike character and virtues. These graces are fundamental if we are to be a bright, shining light—a city set on a hill that cannot be hidden.

Scripture declares that "the righteous shall be as bold as a lion." True boldness stems from a steadfast, upright heart. Our life must be a fountain, filled and overflowing with the fruit of God's Spirit (Galatians 5:22–26).

The desperate cry of many in the church is: **"Oh, Lord let your works appear unto your people"** (Psalms 90:16-17). The good news is God has heard this cry and is responding with true anointing resting upon pure, upright leadership. It is imperative that leadership set a higher standard scripture states as the people so with the priest. Leaders are responsible for setting a proper pattern for their followers, purity of heart is a must, if we are going to behold the Lord see Hebrews 12:14.

These are days of preparation the Lord's people are being groomed to encounter Him in the fiery cloud of His Presence thus receiving insights and strategies for this pivotal season. God will be found of all that are seeking Him with their whole heart see Jeremiah 29:12-13. Truly deep is calling unto deep none should remain half-hearted and shallow now is the time to launch out into the deep see Psalms 42:7. Our main goal is Christlikeness, bearing His image. Our quest is to live each day in such a manner that we are pleasing to the Lord see Col. 1:9-10.

The Spirit of Truth is highlighting purity and uprightness it is so encouraging to see the deep desire in the hearts of so many of God's leadership to walk in true holiness. The marks of maturity are being seen in many lives. God's divine truth is being revealed in the inward parts of the heart not just facts contained in the heard, thus resulting in upright character and life style.

Although this is a process that could take a good deal of time to fully mature, never forget God has been at work preparing us for this day for years. We find ourselves in the mist of great acceleration swift shift is upon us. The Body of Christ is now poised to see this reality in a fresh new day of God's plan. The Spirit of God is doing a new thing we must be prepared to move with Him see Isaiah 48:6-7.

God will release revelatory insights for all who are willing to hear Him with a heart set to obey what He is requesting. We are seeing the early stages beginning, awesome leadership is emerging with a single heart that being to establish the King in His kingdom. God will have Himself a people of purity and power moving in true authority. This is not a time to be hum-drum thinking what is coming is what we have seen before.

As leaders we are to prepare the people because we have never been where we are going now see Joshua 3:4. We are entering into a season of signs and wonders, on a level not experienced in our life time. Christ Jesus will have Himself a people prepared to do greater works see John 14:12.

These will not be super-saints but rather ordinary people anointed with the power of God's Holy Spirit. It is the Spirit of God that has qualified us for this hour of victory. It is not our own efforts but the anointing of God's Spirit that will make the difference.

The Ordinary Saint Anointed with Extraordinary Anointing

Who are these coming leaders? Are they special people with amazing giftings and anointings? Not necessarily, this is one of the deceptions we must erase—that God only uses special people. Nothing could be more distant from Biblical truth (See 1 Corinthians 1:26). These coming leaders were "who so ever will" ? "You could be one of them"?

Remember the Lord is looking for a people whose heart is right with Him, so that He can fully support all that they are doing 11 Chronicles 16:9. The Spirit of Truth is raising up leaders with integrity and character that will teach us the vast difference between what is pure and what is profane (Ezekiel 44:23). We must raise the standard! These are unusual days of destiny and we must arise to the challenge. God is looking for the ordinary saint who's heart is passionately burning for the establishing of the King in His kingdom.

Consequently it is crucial that we walk in uprightness if we are to ascend the hill of the Lord (Psalms 24:4-6). As we embrace accountability, we can be trusted with more true spiritual authority. Christ Jesus informed us that if we are faithful over little we will become ruler over much more (Matthew 25:21). On the other hand, if we fail to handle small things correctly even the small things are in danger of being removed.

A Prophetic Promise from the Lord

In a vivid prophetic experience the Spirit of the Lord spoke these encouraging words to me: "*Accept No Imitations! Expect No Limitations! Embrace Infinite Possibilities!*" As we aspire to make these three directives a living reality in our lives, we will see the church launched into a much higher level of God's power.

Accept No Imitations

Artificial ... counterfeit ... synthetic. These are a few of the words that help us to better understand the word "imitation." I once asked a bank president "How do your tellers detect a counterfeit bill?" His answer was profound "The best way to expose phony money is to be so accustomed to handling the real thing that when you touch a fake, something within you instantly sets off a warning."

This is what the body of Christ must have — true intimacy with Jesus that instantly reveals any imitation. We must become so accustomed to His voice that the enticing stranger's voice does not move us. If we are the sheep of His fold, we must come to know and follow our Shepherd's voice. The world's siren song attempts to lure believers from the heavenly sound that resonates in their spirits. We cannot continue to spend our lives on that which is false and worthless. All wood, hay, and stubble must be removed.

We see the call for apostolic living in the message of the book of Jude. It sounds as a piercing bell to the end-time church age. The warning is all too clear: If we do not return to the Acts of the Apostles we will continue to see the actions of the apostates. It is imperative that we become contenders and defenders of the faith. We are urged to "Contend for the faith that was once for all entrusted to the saints" (Jude 3).

EXPECT NO LIMITATIONS

If we will refuse imitations and walk in an unadulterated relationship with Christ, then we can expect no limitations. Jesus said in Matthew 9:29 **"According to your faith be it unto you."** If we will expect more, God will release more. It is time now to begin to embrace the formation of a character within us that will release God's infinite possibilities.

The world is waiting to see a true display of God's power. It is not enough just to talk about God's awesome actions; we must display them. We discover in 1 Corinthians 4:20 that it was never God's plan to establish His kingdom with mere words, but with power. In Hebrews 11:1 we find that active faith produces two much-needed elements: substance and evidence. The Spirit of God will release upon us living proof of God's power if we are willing to yield ourselves completely to Him. Paul stated in 1 Corinthians 2:1-5 that he did not depend upon enticing words of man's wisdom but rather upon the power of God's Spirit to convince men of their need of Christ. **"'Not by might nor by power, but by My Spirit,' Says the Lord of hosts"** (Zechariah 4:6).

My heart is encouraged by the faith building statements from a precious powerful lady , Kathryn Kuhlman:

- *The only limit to the power of God lies within the individual.*
- *It is when active faith dares to believe God to the point of action that something has to happen.*

Sister Kuhlman walked in an awesome anointing for the supernatural, because she was willing to fully follow the Lord. Only as we lay down our ways and yielded to His way will we truly see the infinite power of God manifested in our life.

EMBRACE INFINITE POSSIBILITIES

In order to embrace someone we must first draw near, reach forth our hand, take hold of Him, and bring Him near to our heart. A true embrace is heart to heart; there is no such thing as a distant embrace. We cannot embrace this coming move of God at a distance. He is calling each of us to draw nearer to Him leaving behind our complacent attitudes. Now is time to come aside, to know His heart. In Psalms 46:10 we are instructed to be still and know that He is the Lord. It is only as we behold His face that we are truly changed into His divine image. To begin this process I encourage you to meditate upon His promises.

Once, the Lord spoke these encouraging words to me: *"If I can find a people without mixture, I will pour out My power without measure."* The book of Revelation 3:20-22 tells us that a group of overcomers will walk in true kingdom power. This causes three questions to arise in my heart: *If not you, who? If not here, where? If not now, when?* I cannot emphasize these questions enough:

"**Why not you**"? Yes, you, the one reading this chapter feeling inadequate and unqualified. Read the Word and cry out to God for more faith. Never forget you are special to God, He only created one in the entire world like you. He desires to use you in a uniquely divine manner.

"**Why not here**"? In your life, your family's life, your workplace, your city. Many feel if they could change their environment then God could use them. However, notice where John was when he had his greatest encounter with the Living Christ, on a rock island serving as a prison (See Revelation 1:9).

"**Why not now**"? Ask God to give you grace to totally abandon yourself to Him and His glorious calling on your life. You will find Him when you search for Him with all your heart (See Jeremiah 29:12).

Genesis 18:14 poses the question **"Is there anything too hard for the Lord?"** The prophet Jeremiah clearly answers: **"Ah, Lord God! Behold, You have made the heaven and the earth by Your great power and outstretched** arm. **There is nothing too hard for You"** (Jeremiah 32:17). The cry of our soul must be — "God, nothing is impossible with You!"

Let's pray for big faith that moves God's hand. Now is the time to think big. God can do anything. It is time to expect more, believe for more, and ask for more. Paul the apostle reminded us that **"God is able to do exceeding abundantly above all we could ask or think according to the power that is at work within each of us"** (Ephesians 3:20–21). I love what Smith Wigglesworth said "There are boundless possibilities for us, if we dare to act in God and dare to believe."

Transition Produces Transformation in Our Lives

Presently, these emerging leaders are in a season of sifting and pruning—the refiner's fire is forging their character to carry this unique anointing. Many feel a sense of disorientation at this time; this is the result of spinning on the "Potter's wheel." Seasons of change never feel comfortable.

However, be assured the Master Potter Himself is about to touch the soft pliable clay, and soon we will bear His image. We are in a time of transition which will produce transformation. Our responsibility is to remain soft and moist—yielded upon the Master's wheel. If we attempt to mold ourselves or if we allow ourselves to become dry and brittle we must be broken and remolded. It is imperative that we stay soft and surrendered before the Lord.

CHARACTER — NOT JUST GIFTING

The refiner's fire is absolutely purifying these leaders so the anointing will not be lost nor the wineskins damaged or destroyed for lack of character. It is required of a steward that he be found faithful. Unfortunately we've seen many tragic examples of great giftings in people who lacked the character needed to steward them appropriately. God will impart the divine nature and holy character established in the Spirit of the Lord. These emerging leaders and counselors will not judge by what their eyes see or what their ears hear, but in true righteousness they will make decisions resulting in equity and justice.

It is crucial for the church to begin walking in true apostolic authority. If we are going to be trusted with a higher level of authority it is essential for us to walk in integrity and uprightness (See Hebrews 12:14). The instructions are extremely clear in I Peter 1:13-16. **"Gird up our mind, speaking of soberness. . . ."** God is serious about His children living upright. Verse 16 states: **"Because it is written, 'Be ye holy; for I am holy.' "** Living clean is not bondage it is true freedom.

Again, let me impress upon each of you the mandate to embrace the promise of purity found in 2 Corinthians 7:1 **"Therefore, having these promises, beloved, let us cleanse ourselves from all filthiness of the flesh and spirit, perfecting holiness in the fear of God."** The results of this embrace will be our identification as sons and daughters of the Almighty God. What an awesome motivation to strive for purity and avoid deception.

The Spirit of Truth is seeking to establish each one of us in truth. Christ Jesus commanded **"Sanctify them in the truth; Your word is truth"** (John 17:17). As believers, we are to have upright lives that are characterized by authentic lifestyles of faith. Our walk must match our talk if we are to have a message that will legitimately change lives. It is time to take a stand for righteousness and holiness. Grace is not a license for loose living.

In our attempts to appear politically correct, have we drifted far from the calling to stand for truth and righteousness? Only as we return to true holiness of heart can we be vessels of honor. This will allow us to be sanctified in truth and be presentable to the Lord as consecrated vessels. The call is clear that we must walk in truth if we are to powerfully present the Truth. We must present the Truth in order for freedom to reign in the hearts' of man.

End-Time Ministry Giftings

part 3

Building Upon a Sure Foundation

The manifold wisdom of God's will be expressed through these anointed vessels as they have labored laying the foundation for the end-time church. Ephesians 2:20 declares: **"Having been built on the foundation of the apostles and prophets, Christ Jesus Himself being the corner stone."** Of course, there is no other foundation laid other than Christ Jesus. Make sure that your foundation is solid we must study the Word of God in order to have this firm foundation.

It is so very encouraging to see the deep hunger for the Word of God arising within the heart of God's people.

Never forget faith comes by hearing and hearing by the Word of God. As I go about the nations I am privileged to minister in many schools of ministry there I am finding young people who have a burning passion for ministry but also a deep hunger to know the Word of God. Truly there is coming a marrigage between the Word and the Spirit. This alone can build a firm foundation.

Christ warned against building upon a faulty foundation. Matthew 7:24-27 informs us that these houses will fall. However, if we build upon the sure foundation of God's revealed Word, our house will withstand any storm. I am asked by people from all across the Body of Christ what God is doing now. I tell them He is tearing down everything we have built that is not Him. He is dismantling all that we have done that is not from Him.

The Prophet for years have been saying that there was coming a merging of the Word and the Spirit we are now seeing this become a living reality.

These end-time leaders will be an expression of the Holy Spirit's work through individuals who embody the merger of the Word and Spirit that produces the life of Christ. We discover in Ephesians 2:20-22 we are to be His holy house. Each of us should strive to keep our lives clean and pure knowing that our body is the temple of the Holy Spirit. See 1 Corinthians 3:16-17 and 1 Corinthians 6:19-20 as Paul pleads with us to be pure. Remember, if the foundation is faulty the entire structure is compromised.

Now that we know the type of righteous living required to attain to these offices, let's look at several of these emerging governmental positions:

Priest, Prophet and Judge

The Prophet Samuel is one of the most vivid examples of the emerging apostolic leadership for this generation. We see Samuel was a gift from God, and a gift given back to God. By understanding his role in Israel's leadership, we can also glean considerable insight into present day apostolic leadership that is being prepared. The Palmist spoke of Samuel and this anointing saying:

Moses and Aaron were among His priests, and Samuel was among those who called on His name; they called upon the LORD and He answered them. He spoke to them in the pillar of cloud; they kept His testimonies and the statute that He gave them (Psalms 99:6-7).

Notice from this passage Samuel was in communication with God, he prayed and God answered. This is a key to true leadership knowing God and following God. This coming leadership will be multi-mantled just as Samuel functioned in Israel as priest, prophet, and judge. He was a man of noble character who also carried the clear manifestation of God's Spirit. His ministry was marked by prophetic accuracy and intimate fellowship with the Lord. As a young child he could hear the voice of the Lord. As a young man he not only heard but he heeded the voice of the Lord.

THE FUNCTION OF THE ANOINTED PRIESTS

The Spirit of God will aid us in grasping a deeper understanding of the term "inspired priests." It is a reference to teachers who receive their understanding of the Word through divine revelation. The Apostle Paul stated that his revelation of the Word came, not by the teaching of man or by reading a book, but by a divine revelation of Jesus Christ (See 2 Corinthians 12:1-5).

The Spirit of Truth will anoint these inspired teachers that are coming and they will promote a message of sanctification within the church. Consecrated believers are a suitable dwelling place for God's Spirit and they will become partakers of His divine nature and Holy character (See Ezekiel 44:15-16; 23-24).

The fruit of the Spirit is a prerequisite for the release and impartation of the power gifts and God's highest callings, which are necessary for end-time ministry. In Acts 1:8 we are informed that the Holy Spirit releases power for a purpose and that purpose is to get the message of God's redemptive grace to a hurting world. Never forget we preach a better message with our life than our lips. If we are not living it people will not want to hear what we have to say.

Another predominant function of the inspired teachers will be to Biblically communicate the Lord's requirements for the end-time generation. Through their revelation of the Word by the Spirit of Truth, they will teach the church consecration in order to be viable participants in the glorious ministry yet to come. A biblical model of this is the Zadok priests.

THE FUNCTION OF THE ZADOK PRIESTHOOD

The Spirit of God is releasing many insights about the role and the responsibility of the Zadok Priesthood. The Spirit of Truth is calling for each of us to walk in their anointing. They had the responsibility of modeling and maintaining the highest standards of morality, self-control, and self-denial. They were charged with teaching the people how to distinguish between what was Godly and ungodly so no deception would lead the people astray. **"Moreover, they shall teach My people the difference**

between the holy and the profane, and cause them to discern between the unclean and the clean" (Ezekiel 44:23).

These emerging, anointed priests will begin to authenticate that which is holy and expose that which is profane. What is the difference between the profane and the holy? The Lord said what He called profane was anything we are doing that He did not initiate. Remember Christ's words **"I never knew you, depart from Me you workers of iniquity"?** (Matthew 7:23). He said this to a person who had been very involved in religious activity, but did not truly trust Christ.

There is a vast difference between deception and denial. Many people today are walking in deception because they do not know that they have departed from the path of righteousness. Those who embrace the call to the Zadok priesthood will be used by God to unveil deception. However, many are also aware of their wanderings, but refuse to admit that they have turned away from their first love. Only those who become genuine, authentic, and unadulterated in their walk with Him will inherit the powerful and precious promises God is pouring out to His end-time church.

Another fundamental function of the Zadok priesthood is to minister unto the Lord as described in Ezekiel 44:15–16:

> *"But the priests, the Levites, the sons of Zadok, who kept charge of My sanctuary when the children of Israel went astray from Me, they shall come near Me to minister to Me; and they shall stand before Me to offer Me the fat and the blood...." says the Lord God. "They shall enter My sanctuary, and they shall come near My table to minister to Me, and they shall keep My charge."*

This signifies an emphasis on the five-fold ministry of prophetic teachers. Notice in the above passage these leaders were in charge of MY sanctuary and they shall come near MY table to minister to ME. This is the key to all true ministry; it must first be to the Lord. This will be the guideline for the coming leadership as they prepare the body of Christ to receive the strong prophetic and apostolic ministries yet to be truly inaugurated. Expect to see leadership go to a whole new level.

The Prophets

The prophets are another essential end-time ministry group. Their primary purpose will be to reveal the 12 primary redemptive natures of God. These attributes were expressed through Jehovah of the Old Testament and Jesus of the New Testament. All of the redemptive natures of Jehovah were found in the person of Jesus Christ who is our ultimate expression of the Father. In Colossians 1:15 we discover that Christ Jesus is the expressed image of the invisible God.

Even as Revelations 22:2 expresses the 12 manner of fruit from the tree of life bearing in their proper seasons, so shall the Holy Spirit reveal to the church the 12 primary redemptive natures of Christ and their proper Biblical applications. We will look at these 12 primary redemptive natures of God later in great detail.

EVIDENCE OF SPIRITUAL LEADERSHIP

As the church matures and moves toward perfection, we will begin to see the priesthood in the order of Melchizedek emerging. He was the king of Salem and priest of the Most High God. We know from scripture that He was none other than God veiled in human flesh revealing Himself to Abraham. See Genesis 14:17 and Hebrews 7:11 to gain a better understand of the order of Melchizedek's priesthood.

THEIR IDENTIFICATION

They will manifest the Fruit of the Spirit. **"But the fruit of the Spirit is love, joy, peace, longsuffering, kindness, goodness, faithfulness, gentleness, self-control. Against such there is no law"** (Galatians 5:22-23).

The surest evidence of God's true leadership in a believer,

even more important than the Spirit's power gifts, is the revelation of the fruit of the Spirit through a consecrated life of righteousness. I talked earlier about the necessity of bearing the fruit of the Spirit. This is only achieved by the Holy Spirit abiding in us. When this happens believers will become partakers of the divine nature that reveals the Spirit of Holiness.

Christ stated that His followers would be known by their fruit. The greatest evidence of the anointing is the manifestation of the life of Christ revealed by the fruit of the Spirit. It is reported concerning the early disciples that they were unlearned but that people took notice of them because they had been with Jesus (See Acts 4:13). Oh, how we need to become more and more like HIM! This can become a reality by obeying the promise of 2 Corinthians 3:18 **"But we all, with unveiled face, beholding as in a mirror the glory of the Lord, are being transformed into the same image from glory to glory, just as by the Spirit of the Lord."**

The evidence of His character in us is ultimately pleasing to the Lord. These emerging men and women will not only be known by their fruit, but their purpose will be to manifest God's redemptive attributes in the earth.

THEIR ANOINTING

Their anointing will come from Isaiah 11:2, the sevenfold Spirit of God. **"The Spirit of the LORD shall rest upon Him, The Spirit of wisdom and understanding, The Spirit of counsel and might, The Spirit of knowledge and of the fear of the LORD."** The seven Spirits of God are the full manifestations of the Holy Spirit flowing in the life of Christ Jesus.

God is looking for end-time leadership that will truly bear the image of Christ Jesus. They will bear the Spirit of wisdom and revelation, and bring understanding concerning the seven Spirits of God and their importance to the overcoming church now being prepared. Great will be the blessing of all who overcome. They will, according to

Revelation 2:17, be able to eat the hidden manna and obtain a white stone, thus revealing that God's favor is manifested upon their life.

Their Purpose

To reveal the 12 names illustrating the divine character of God and His primary redemptive attributes manifested in the person of Jesus.

Once in a powerful prophetic encounter Christ stated to me that the sum of His earthly ministry can be seen in John 17:6 which states **"Father I have manifested your name."** I did not fully understand what He was attempting to teach me. The truth is that in the Old Testament Father God identified Himself in covenant reverential names and Christ came and gave fleshly form and function to each of these names. Proverbs 18:10 assures us that the name of the Lord is a strong tower where the righteous can run for safety. God has also said He has esteemed His word above His name.

I'm closing this chapter with the teaching on the names of God from a very trusted friend of mine, Paul Keith Davis, founder of Whitedove Ministries. Your spiritual walk will be greatly blessed by his insights. I trust you will visit his outstanding web site at www.whitedoveministries.org. His article is printed by permission from the author. These are the names that the coming leadership will reveal.

THE REDEMPTIVE NAMES OF GOD

By Paul Keith Davis

Jehovah Rohi – 'The Lord my shepherd' is from Psalm 23:1. After leaving Egypt, Israel learned to magnify the Lord for life, healing, victory, holiness, peace, and protection. However, they were still in need of divine provision in their wilderness journey. Thus there came the revelation of God as their Jehovah Rohi, the One whose Shepherd love, care and resources they could depend upon in the unknown future pathways. Thus the Lord is the feeder to provide, keeper to protect, companion to cheer, friend to help, pastor to comfort and herdsman near to us, as His frequent revelations prove.

Jehovah Jireh – 'The Lord will provide' is found in Genesis 22:14. The definition of this term is "The Lord will see" or "The Lord will provide." For man this conjunctive meaning seems impossible. However, for the all-knowing God of creation the dual meaning is easily exemplified.

His pre-vision means His pro-vision. That was Abraham's revelation when he found the ram provided as Isaac's substitute. This was God's creative miracle for the sacrifice in the same sense that God created a body through the miraculous conception for Jesus' substitutionary sacrifice. As Elohim, God demanded Isaac's sacrifice, but as Jehovah He made complete provision of a substitute for the son Abraham willingly offered.

Jehovah Tsidkenu – 'The Lord our righteousness' is found in Jeremiah 33:16. The glory of the gospel is that Jehovah Tsidkenu became flesh and was made righteousness for us (1 Corinthians. 1:30). A righteous God pronounced death as the penalty of sin, yet that righteous God became flesh, to taste death for every sinner and provide the righteousness that is imputed to the believer and is accepted before God. Acceptable righteousness is not attained but obtained.

Jehovah Shalom – The Lord our peace is used in Judges 6:42. The word "peace" and its cognates appear over 400 times in scripture. It is one of the most precious and fundamentally essential ingredients for a believer to be at peace with and know the peace of God. It relates to a harmonious relationship obtained through reconciliation of a debt paid in full. Peace or "Shalom" is often translated as welfare, good health, prosperity, favor, rest, whole, finished, restitution or repay and perfect.

Jehovah Rophi – 'The Lord our physician,' is from Exodus 15:26, where we learn that in times of sickness God heals. To express God's grace in restoring spirit life, He declared that He healed all of our diseases, spiritual as well as physical (Psalms 103:3; Genesis 20:17; Matthew 4:23). He also is the one who heals the broken hearted (Psalms 147:3) and for those who are backsliding, He is their healer as well (Jeremiah 3:22).

Jehovah Nissi – 'The Lord our banner' is found in Exodus 17:15-16. Moses took care that God should have the glory for the victory over Amalek. Instead of setting up a trophy in Joshua's honor, though this had been standard practice, instead he built an altar to God's honor. What is most carefully recorded is the inscription upon the altar, "Jehovah-Nissi - The Lord my Banner." The presence and power of Jehovah was the banner under which they were enlisted and by which they were kept together.

Jehovah Nissi in literal Hebrew means, "A hand upon the throne of Jehovah." Jehovah will have war with Amalek from generation to generation. Amalek's hand had dared to assault Jehovah's throne to overturn it and so He gave Israel the authority and power of that throne to overwhelm Amalek. The uplifted hands of Moses symbolized this banner. Here we have an illustration of the hand of faith outstretched in prayer.

Jehovah M'Kaddesh – 'The Lord who sanctifies' is from Exodus 31:13. The term holiness is from the Hebrew word "Kodesh" and is allied to "sanctify" and is translated as dedicate, consecrate, hallow and holy in various translations. This term's main influence relates to moral and spiritual purity.

In the New Testament many scriptures relate to the process of sanctification provided to the church through the atoning work of Christ: Sanctified by truth (John 15:3; 17:17), Sanctified by blood (Hebrews 13:12), Sanctified by Faith (Acts 26:18), and Sanctified by prayer (I Timothy 4:5).

While these nine names above are fairly well known, there are four more that are not as common. Let's learn about them now:

Jehovah Tsebahoth – 'The Lord of hosts' is the Hebrew

term from 1 Samuel 1:3 taken from sabaoth, meaning host or hosts with special reference to warfare, armies or service. It often appears as the Lord of Hosts. This reference for Jehovah appears fourteen times in Haggai and twenty-four times in Malachi.

In Zechariah, the Lord of Hosts, occurs fifty-three times and is connected with God's action in judgment and blessing upon Israel. The expression, "Thus saith the Lord of Hosts" implied divine revelation and divine authority.

When the conquest of Canaan was about to begin the Lord was revealed as the unknown warrior with drawn sword standing before Joshua. When Joshua asked the question "Are you for us or against us?" The reply came, "I am Prince of the Host of Jehovah" therefore Joshua humbly surrendered his sword to Jehovah Tsebahoth (See Joshua 5:13-15).

The whole of His creation is under His control and obeys His sovereign command, willingly or otherwise.

He is: The Lord of all angelic hosts (I Kings 22:19), The Lord of all stellar regions (Genesis 1:16), The Lord of all the feathered hosts (I Kings 17:2-7), The Lord of all the animal hosts (Isaiah 11:6), The Lord of all the human hosts (Isaiah 40:15) and The Lord of the satanic hosts (Matthew 28:18).

Jehovah Heleyon – 'The Lord Most High' is found in Isaiah. 57:15 and is frequently used in the Psalms as a declaration of God's highest position or kingship. God is the high and lofty one that inhabits eternity. It prophetically speaks of Jehovah's earthly reign at the time of Israel's restoration or the restoration of God's chosen people.

During these difficult days it is reassuring to know that that the Most High also rules in the kingdom of men (Daniel 4:25). This redemptive name places God at the highest place of every realm so that He can fulfill His will in and through us. This redemptive name reveals that though He is the highest, there are others below Him endowed by Him with like natures and related to Him by His Spirit.

Jehovah-Makkeh – 'The Lord who smites' is from Ezekiel 7:9. The Lord set Israel in the midst of heathen nations as His witness. But instead of revealing Him, Israel practiced great wickedness. Therefore He said, "You shall know that I am Jehovah-Makkeh, the Lord who smites thee" (Ezekiel 7:9).

In Daniel the 9th chapter Israel found themselves in captivity because they refused to heed the Lord's voice through the prophets. As a result the Lord disciplined Israel. The church has also experienced a similar disciplinary period over the past forty years because of her rejection of the true revealed word as brought to the church by His servants, the prophets.

The good news is His promise to restore. Hosea 6:1-2, states,

> *Come, let us return to the LORD. For He has torn us but He will heal us; He has wounded us but He will*

bandage us. He will revive us after two days; He will raise us up on the third day, that we may live before Him.

Jehovah Gmolah – 'The God of recompense' is in Jeremiah 51:6. The scriptures declare that retribution or recompense does not belong to us but to God. In Jeremiah 51:6 the Lord declares that He will severely punish Babylon because of their harsh dealing with Israel, thereby revealing Himself as the God of retribution. The same was true of Egypt when they placed Israel under a heavy burden.

When we are shamefully treated or misjudged it becomes very difficult not to take up our own defense, but to leave our reputation to God. Yet this is precisely what He has instructed. Retribution and recompense belong only to Him. Vengeance is His and He promised to repay (Deuteronomy 32:35; II Thessalonians 1:8).

Jehovah Shammah – 'The Lord is there' is from Ezekiel 48:35. The name of the city revealed through Ezekiel is

Jehovah Shammah. This location is so named because of the manifest presence and power of Jehovah residing therein. We also know from scripture that God does not dwell in temples made by hands, but rather we are to be God's temple.

The apostle Paul describes the church as a habitation of God, a house of God, and the building growing unto a holy temple in the Lord. The question remains: Does the Glory of Jehovah fill His house, and are we, members of that house, displaying His Glory?

This is the last of Jehovah's redemptive titles in the order of their Old Testament occurrence. It discloses the consummation of His progressive self-revelation.

THE
CONSECRATION
OF OUR MIND

part 4

Heaven, as well as hell is posing the identical question to each person in the Body of Christ. The question being asked by both the Spirit of God and the devil is: "Who do you think you are"?

Our failure to properly distinguish who God has truly called and commissioned us to be has had devastating results. Many are living in exile, distant from the provisions and position God has called them to obtain. Satan is a master thief. He will do all within his power to steal your destiny so you will live in spiritual poverty and constant lack. God's plans for you are to be the head and not the tail to be above and not below (See Deuteronomy 28:13). God has destined you to be victorious not a victim.

Never become content settling for less than God's highest goal for your life. As followers of Christ each of us is called to become the "manifested Sons and Daughters of Almighty God." If we settle for anything less than this we are living short of our divine destiny. Our highest goal is to be like the Lord Jesus in everyway; conformed to the image of Christ. Romans 8:29 **"For whom He foreknew, He also predestined to be conformed to the image of His Son...."**

We are in a season of revelation of truth; this truth will set us free to be all God has called us to be. Christ said **"You shall know the truth and the truth shall set you free"** (John 8:32). We are called to walk in the light not stumble in the darkness.

Much of our destiny hinges upon our clear understanding of who we truly are. This is not a time for wrong assessment. We must know for certain who God has set us apart to be. This is plainly displayed in the history of Israel as they refused to believe God had given them the Promised Land.

When they looked with their natural eyes their eye of faith was dimmed. Then they attempted to figure out with their natural minds how to acquire the promise. Numbers 13:33 tells us that because they perceived themselves as weak grasshoppers the enemy also saw them weak and unqualified.

The foe of our soul is unrelenting. He never stops his attack. The battlefield for our soul is the mind. The scriptures reveal that what we fix our mind upon will set the course for our lifestyle. As a person thinks within his heart so will be the direction of his life. It is important to fill your soul with the promises of God such as Joel 3:10b. **"Let the weak say 'I am strong.' "** or Nahum 1:7 **"God is good and a very present help in the time of trouble."**

We are called and commissioned to live by the control of the Spirit (See Romans 8:1-2). If we walk according to the flesh, we find great difficulty. However if we are lead by the Holy Spirit, God will give great grace to our life. Only then are we truly free to become all God has purposed us to be. If we are going to change our lifestyle we must first change our mind-set. We need a true "brain-washing" in order to rid ourselves of stinking thinking. We must have the mind of Christ. A clear, clean mind; thinking on things that are good and honest and fixing our thoughts on proper things (See Philippians 4:8-9).

NATURAL VERSUS SPIRITUAL MIND

In 2 Corinthians, Paul contrasts two kinds of minds, the natural mind, and the spiritual mind. The natural mind is a mind dull and darkened to spiritual things, however brilliant it might be in its own natural sphere.

It is possible to be a child of God and yet, be largely dominated by the laws of the natural mind. Paul's prayer emphasizes the desperate need for a spirit-enlightened mind for the Ephesians. **That the God of our Lord Jesus Christ, the Father of glory, may give to you the Spirit of wisdom and revelation in the knowledge of Him: The eyes of your understanding being enlightened that you**

may know… (Ephesians 1:17, 18a).

It matters not how brilliant a person might be--he cannot understand the things of God with the natural mind. **"The natural man receives not the things of the Spirit of God: for they are foolishness to him: neither can he know them, because they are spiritually discerned"** (1 Corinthians 2:14). Attempting to figure out the moves of the Spirit of God by natural means and the natural mind will always end in failure. Our prayer must be for God to open the eyes of our heart so that we can grasp what He is doing.

In Leviticus 1:8 we discover an example of having a consecrated mind; when the children of Israel brought a "voluntary offering" to the Lord, they were to lay the head of the offering upon the altar. This is a vivid reminder that we too must have our minds renewed by communion with the Lord. We too must have our mind renewed and cast upon the altar. Ask the Spirit of God to search out every negative aspect of your heart, only then can you walk clean and free from deception (See Psalms 139:23).

This is not a season to be at ease and loose about our lifestyle. We are to pursue peace and holiness, for without a pure and holy life we will not see God (See Hebrews 12:14. God is calling His people to walk in purity. A strong promise is revealed in 2 Corinthians 7:1. **"Therefore, having these promises, beloved, let us cleanse ourselves from all filthiness of the flesh and spirit, perfecting holiness in the fear of God."** We are called to complete consecration of both body and spirit. Only as we seek to maintain clean hands and a pure heart can we expect to draw near to God (See Psalms 24:4-5).

Don't misunderstand me; I am not suggesting that we never depend upon our intellectual wisdom to advance us in the realm of the Holy Spirit. It is to the humble, simple minded person God reveals great grace.

Be Humble and Childlike

The truly humble people receive things that are hidden from the wise. This concept caused the heart of Christ to rejoice, knowing that the things of God were freely revealed to all who truly seek. We cannot approach God with just our natural mind, our intelligence. Notice Matthew 11:25 **"At that time Jesus answered and said, 'I thank You, O Father, Lord of heaven and earth, because You have hid these things from the wise and prudent, and have revealed them to babes.' "** It is to the open-hearted child-like person that sacred secrets can be revealed.

Actually God calls ordinary people and anoints them with an extraordinary anointing to accomplish outstanding displays of His power, so that He is the One who gets the glory. Paul makes this very clear in 1 Corinthians 1:26. We are to be child-like not childish. This is not immaturity but rather a teachable, tender heart and gentle spirit. This is what it means to be child like.

As a child we must come to our Heavenly Father totally trusting in His faithfulness and knowing that He has our very best interest in mind (See Jeremiah 29:11). We discover in Isaiah 55:9 **"For as the heavens are higher than** the earth, so are My ways higher than your ways, and My thoughts than your thoughts."

FROM HEAD TO HEART TO HAND

The Spirit of God will move the word of God from the head to the heart to the hands. We will become doers of the Word not just those content to hear (See James 1:22). As revelation of His word increases in believers' lives, they will be impacted to do the work of the Lord cheerfully and with grateful hearts.

God's Word warned in Hosea's day **"My people are destroyed for lack of knowledge"** (Hosea 4:6a). He was not speaking of a lack of "secular" knowledge, but of a lack of the "spiritual" knowledge of God. Now is the time to embrace Paul's prayer in Colossians 1:6-12. He prayed for our "spiritual understanding to increase." Line your mind up with God's word.

It is one thing to know about God, yet quite another thing to know God. Just as it is one thing to know about a popular person, and quite another thing to personally know that person. A strong warning is released by Christ Jesus in Matthew 7:23 **"I never knew you...."**

A person can store up theological facts, while the God of these facts may mean very little to them. Facts obtained in the head and not experienced in the heart can lead to a powerless spirit of religion that promotes legalism.

Our quest is to yield our mind to be illuminated by the Holy Spirit, thus transforming the way we think about all things. As followers of Christ every facet of our lives must be directed by the Spirit of God. Whatever we do in word or deed we are to do for the Glory of God.

This illumination can only take place as the Holy Spirit "renews" our minds, without which we are incapable of proving **"What is that good, and acceptable, and perfect, will of God"** (Romans 12:2b).

Human Logic versus the Spirit

The natural mind can be a menace, particularly in the realm of the spirit. God's ways seem diametrically opposed to "common sense." The warning is clear – **"There is a way**

that seems right unto a man however that is the ways of death" (Proverbs 16:25). The only way to true wisdom is to apply the teaching of the Word of God to our daily life.

The unspiritual mind of the unspiritual man has done, and is still doing enormous harm to the church. It encroaches into a sphere in which it has no part, and tries to insert the authority of its own logic into a realm in which it has no competence.

The man with the unspiritual mind is not satisfied with the Scriptural parameter of what are commonly called the "Gifts of the Spirit." Therefore, he makes his own judgment regarding the authoritative criterion of the working of the Holy Spirit, until he regulates the "Gifts of the Spirit" out of the church. It is extremely dangerous to attribute the works of God's Holy Spirit to the devil. Having become wise in his own opinion, the unspiritual man substitutes for, and finally denies, the spiritual operations and manifestations of the Gifts of the Holy Spirit. We must be careful not to exercise our options above the teaching of Christ.

One of the ways to spot man-made controlled religion is the presence of rituals that substitute man's ways instead of God's ways: feasting for fasting, ritual for real Christian life, and gratification of self life for a true visitation of God's Spirit, substituting the seeker friendly, super soft message in place of the power of the cross, compromise for courage and human psychology for spiritual discernment. A person who depends upon his own efforts substitutes human zeal in the place of Heaven's anointing. This is not the mind of Christ. He will present Christianity as sugar instead of salt, and solicit the praise of men rather than the honor of God.

We must remember the stern warning from the lips of our Lord **"Without Me you can do nothing"** (John 15:5). All that is done without the leadership of the Spirit is wood, hay and stubble and destined for the fire. We should pray that fire would refine our works now to make sure we are building upon the firm foundation of Christ and His Word. Only these works will abide.

GOD'S WISDOM VERSUS MAN'S "WISDOM"

The Word of God reveals the knowledge of His ways, in contrast to our own ways. God is not restricted to man's mere methods. There is a strong questions posed in Genesis 18:14. **"Is there anything too hard for God?"** The answer to this question is revealed in Luke 1:37 which states that with men things are impossible however with God nothing is impossible. God might not do things like we think He should, however, He is never wrong.

This principal is dramatically set forth in the battle of Jericho (Joshua 6). Being a walled city, it defied any natural means at the Israelites' disposal. God did not provide scaling ladders, battering rams, and the like. Instead, God gave Joshua instructions which were, from a natural point of view, totally ludicrous. The Israelites were to walk around the city once a day for six days, and seven times on the seventh day then shout and blow trumpets. They were to walk without saying a word and then at the appointed time to shout.

God's method called for an obedient faith, regardless of the outrageous insult to common sense and the reasoning of the natural mind. What an incredible sight this must have been; seasoned Israelite warriors weakened by their recent circumcisions hiking around this massive wall under the scowls and hisses of the opposing army. Never forget God's ways are higher than our ways yet His ways are always right. If we learn to fully follow God's ways we will be successful.

God Not Limited by Human Judgment

God is not constrained to man's choices. God knows the end from the beginning. He is Author and Finisher not Author and Oops! Nothing catches God by surprise. **"For the Lord sees not as man sees; for man looks on the outward appearance, but the Lord looks on the heart"** (1 Samuel 16:7b).

In the call and commissioning of an instrument, human judgment may be based upon a consideration of "apparent credentials," or the appeal to the human eye, as in the case of the selection of a King for Israel. God regarded neither experience, rank, nor seniority. He chose the youngest instead of the eldest, a stripling with a heart for God, in preference to a man with an attractive countenance and impressive stature. Eliab appeared to be the right choice but was rejected by the Lord for David. **"And it came to pass, when they were come, that he looked on Eliab, and said, Surely the Lord's anointed is before Him"** (1 Samuel 16:6).

God, in His superior wisdom and knowledge, may by-pass the most likely choice, and instead, reach out for an instrument which man would reject. This is also seen when God appoints Paul an Apostle to the Gentiles and Peter an Apostle to the Jewish followers. This seems to be totally opposite of what should have been done.

Appearances may be deceitful and our own understanding inadequate, therefore, we are admonished to **"Trust in the Lord with all your heart; and lean not unto your own understanding"** (Proverbs 3:5).

God is not Limited to Man's Means

Still another point we must grasp is that God is not limited to man's means. The inadequacy of man's own means, in contrast to those of God, is taught throughout the Bible. It is permanently written on the pages of the history of the church, and constantly demonstrated in experience. Yet man still prefers the glitter and polish of his own machinery, to the humble simplicity of God's provision. It is so easy to forget that the Lord's battles are not won by the might of numbers, nor by the power of human means, but by the "Spirit of the Lord."

God can use the humblest to accomplish the greatest end and frequently chooses the foolish things of the world to confound the wise. **"God hath chosen the weak things of the world, … and things which are despised hath God chosen, yea, and things which are not, to bring to naught the things that are: That no flesh should glory in His presence"** (1 Corinthians 1:27-29). God does not limit Himself to man's means. Scripture states that God's strength is made perfect in our weakness, likewise when we are weak then He is revealed as strong. The Lord always responds to a hungry heart. **"The people who know their God shall be strong, and carry out great exploits"** (Daniel 11:32).

The key to living in victory is remembering that **"Now, we have received, not the spirit of the world, but the spirit which is of God; that we might know the things that are freely given to us of God"** (1 Corinthians 2:12). We should not be stumbling about in the darkness of our logical thinking but rather living in the light knowing through the scriptures what God has promised to provide. Meditate on those scriptures until you know who you are in Christ! The Lord is still seeking those who will accept and submit to His ways.

INSIGHTS INTO THE UNFOLDING PURPOSE OF THE LORD

For the last several years the Holy Spirit has been fanning the flames of discontentment causing God's people to become extremely hungry to know Him. The cry from their lips, echoed across the earth is **"Oh, Lord rend the heavens and come down"** (Isaiah 64:1). There is also desperation to see God's mighty power demonstrated in our day. All across the Body of Christ I hear the plea "Lord, let Your works appear."

Ask yourself these questions: Are you truly desperate for the Living God? Are you gripped with a hunger to know Him, not just in your head but in your heart? Do you want to become unyielding in your pursuit to move into the reality of His divine Presence?

It is time for us to walk in active faith that will produce true evidence and substance (See Hebrews 11:1). God declared He would pour water upon the thirsty and satisfy the hungry soul see Isaiah 44:3-4. The promise is to the desperate and truly hungry they will be filled see Matthew 5:6. I am not talking about some new church program; I am talking about a radical revolution that will redefine our understanding of Christianity. God never intended to establish His kingdom with mere words but with demon-strated power (See 1 Corinthians 4:20).

A Holy Spiritual Journey

We are on a quest to truly know God and now is the time to go deeper in the Holy Spirit. Deep is calling unto the deep; the cry of our heart is **"Oh, God let your works appear"** (Psalms 90:16-17). As the Spirit of God awakens our ears to hear and our eyes to see, we will discover an expansive field of spiritual reality before us and we are to venture there with the Holy Spirit. Now is the time to unlock hidden treasures. Heaven is shouting "No hesitation." Don't wait. It is time to move confidently into God's promises.

The journey to draw near is a quest we must accept with great joy. Our "present attainment" of spiritual life and hunger is initiated by the Lord. He alone can create the deep hunger to know Him more. During these days of swift and sure change God is greatly increasing the hunger to know Him and to become more and more like Him. As we obey the Word of God we find ourselves moving ever deeper into the will of God.

The Spirit of Truth is exceptionally busy building the Body of Christ, training it and doing a thousand things within and through it, so in "that day" we will be a beautiful Bride to be presented to our Lord. The Spirit of Truth is releasing to us a deeper hunger to understand more concerning the majesty of the Master.

Truly we are in a season of preparation like none before. All this is a preliminary training school for the days to come. This spiritual hunger rests on certain levels of spiritual obedience and experience, each level taking us farther. Our quest will not be complete until we bear His image. Thus, there is a continual, progressive development in our spiritual living, moving us from one place of discovery and life, on into another level of discovery and divine life. The more we become like Him the more we desire to be more like Him.

God longs to display His awesome power through a pure people. This speaks of "the spiritual ascent of our being back to the heart of God." Each day we are to experience God's divine nature being made real in our life. It is time to get our priorities in order; this world is not our home. We are here for just a few fleeting years of training and discipline, and then we will be taken. Our life here is training for reigning.

The Holy Spirit of God indwells each true Believer releasing for them power to live the Christian life (See Ezk. 36:27. The promise is clear (See Acts 1:8) that the Holy Spirit, abiding in each believer, releases power.

"It is God that is at work within us both to will and to do His good pleasure" (Philippians 2:13). This is an overwhelming thought that we could actually do something that would bring God good pleasure. Nothing could be more important than living in such a manner as to please our Heavenly Father. We discover in Luke 12:32 that God receives good pleasure finding a people in whom He can release His kingdom. He is looking for such a people (See 2 Chronicles 16:9).

The day is coming when we will cast our crowns at His feet. He alone is worthy to receive glory and honor. This crown is made up of all our godly actions and all that we have become, so that we may be presented to the Lord of Glory as the Bride of Christ, clean and spotless.

God is at work establishing us to be willing warriors. That which has been acquired through discipline and training--through the surrender of our old life to the resurrection of the new--will be projected upon another (higher) plane of living in the days to come.

Having been touched by eternal truth we are seeking to fully follow the Lord; it is important that we have a correct perspective and goal. We are admonished to walk with aim and purpose in these end-times (See Ephesians 5:14-15).

Whatever we build up of spiritual value, vigor, and vision is because we are created in Christ Jesus unto good works (See Ephesians 2:10). Having an upright life is extremely important. Our life must back up what our lips speak. It as been well said we preach a clearer message with our life than our lips.

HIGHER SPIRITUAL GROUND

Each day we should be taking steps toward spiritual maturity. We are to continually move from one level of spiritual understanding and experience to another. This is determined by the amount of spiritual illumination that we have obtained through our responses to the Lord's presence, revelation of the Word by the Spirit and His workings within us.

Then He will guide our path as He disciplines and trains us in order to push us into a higher order of spiritual reality and life. Our upward progress in this will be determined by our degree of spiritual hunger and obedience. The Lord alone can create this spiritual hunger. Our part is to remind the Lord through prayer of the possibilities that He intends for us and walk through the doors as He opens them.

We become spiritually hungry on different levels, according to our commitment and desire toward the Lord. Sometimes people say "Oh, I know that--tell me something new." But first, we must experience the depths of the Word we heard. We must come to realize that there are a thousand facets of light in this glorious gem of redemption, which radiate from it continually. We cannot possess all of this light and illumination now because our capacity of reception has not yet been fully enlarged.

Revelation is a progressive seeking to known Christ Jesus in a deeper way. It is eternally moving and is inexhaustible. This lovely field of spiritual life and experience that is before us is immense, emancipating, and liberating.

We must always remember that the Word of God is active and alive. The more you study it the more you understand the heart of Father God. Jesus did not say "I have some truth to share." Rather, Jesus said, He was *the truth*." All truth is personified in Him and has become articulate and fully expressive in this dynamic, marvelous, living

Christ. The nearer we get to Him, the more we will love Him. There are profound unfoldings by the Spirit into the person of Christ **"In whom are hidden all the treasures of wisdom and knowledge..."** (Colossians 2:3).

All truth is summed up in this revelation: **"He that has seen Me has seen the Father..."** (John 14:9). He is not talking about seeing a body, but rather, the nature and character of God as seen in Jesus. This invisible and marvelous God became visible and articulate in this wonderful dynamic Person, God the Son, eternally identified with us.

Those who gathered around Jesus heard Him speak and saw His miracle power. They were the recipients of His grace and healing, but not even the disciples had a full revelation as to His identity.

After Peter identified Him as the Christ, Jesus said that He had come to this understanding through a direct revelation from the Father. Now the disciples were ready to be lifted into a new level of revelation. He told them that He would die on the cross and He revealed His glory to Peter, James, and John on the Mount of Transfiguration.

With the Apostle Paul, may each of us pray,

> *That I may know Him, and the power of His resurrection, and the fellowship of His sufferings, being conformed to His death; in order that I may attain to the resurrection from the dead. Not that I have already obtained it, or have already become perfect. "But I press on in order that I may lay hold of that for which also I was laid hold of by Christ Jesus"*
>
> (PHILIPPIANS 3:10-12, NAS).

When I began to seek the Lord Himself, I discovered that each unfolding of spiritual truth lead me to a fuller revelation and understanding of Jesus. I have been awakened to this lovely truth and Jesus is becoming an increasing reality in my life. There is much that we already possess but there is much more that is evasive within this Christ. This is where I get blessed, as the Holy Spirit takes me into this "darkness" for a glimpse of something within this marvelous Jesus, who is the Truth.

WALKING IN VICTORY

The Spirit of God is encouraging each of us to "advance." We are commanded to be bold and brave and very courageous (See Joshua 1:7), while moving in power to take the Kingdom for the King! This is not a season to compromise. Walk with clean hands and a pure heart, drawing closer to your Lord. Walk in dominion and power; lay hold of God's promises. This is not a time to be weak but to be bold. The Spirit of God is calling forth the "dread champions."

Listen with your whole heart and take courage. God has promised victory. **"Greater is He that is within you than he that is in the world"** (1 John 4:4). You are created for victory, now is the time to stand up and declare the proclamation found in Micah 3:8 **"Truly I am full of power by the Spirit of the Lord!"**

We are in the harvest of the end of the ages when both the seeds of good and evil are coming to full fruit. **"The Kingdom of Heaven suffers violence and the violent**

take it by force" (Matthew 11:12). God is calling for us to arise and take a strong stand against the works of darkness. We are to take the land. This victory will be accomplished by individuals as well as the corporate church. The end-time church will be a people of demonstrated power (See 2 Corinthians 2:1-5). It is time to see a true demonstration of the power of God's Spirit.

Join with the plea of Psalms 90:16: **"Lord, let your works appear...."** The church should be hungry and desperate to see the works of the Lord. I am weary of seeing the plans and purposes of man. I long to see the mighty acts of God. The Spirit of Truth is calling for us to come into the presence of the Lord.

No one will have an excuse. The way is clear. Anyone of us can advance. The invitation is extended **"Come up here..."** (Revelation 4:1). As we answer the call to enter the door that is standing open in Heaven, we can see clearer and hear more plainly, making the most of our divine call.

This is not a time to wander around the mountain of defeat and unbelief. We are to take God at His word and stand firm in faith. We will become doers of the Word and not just those content to hear. We are called to be over-comers not to be overcome. Never forget God has promised that no weapon formed against you can prosper (See Isaiah 54:17).

The Body of Christ stands poised at the very verge of the greatest move of God in the history of mankind. Each of us should expect swift and radical change. We do not have extra time. We must enter into the promises of God. No matter how confused and confounded we have been in the past, now we can begin to cease from our wilderness wanderings and seek first the kingdom of God.

Paul prayed that we would **"Walk worthy of the Lord being fruitful and increasing in the knowledge and wisdom of the Lord"** (Colossians 1:9-12). Our highest goal must be to advance the King in His kingdom. Our prayer each day must be "on earth as it is in Heaven." We must have a swift synchronization between our walk and Heaven's will. We must have a clear focus.

It is imperative that we feast deeply in God's Word. This will bring about the freedom we need to draw near the Lord. It is as we truly behold Him with an unveiled face that we are changed into His likeness (See 2 Corinthians 3:18). We must walk in freedom. Jesus said that you shall know the Truth and the Truth shall make you free (See John 18:32). Spend time daily meditating upon the Word of God. Let it get deep within your soul and then you will experience its transforming effect (See Psalms 19:7-14).

If knowing the truth in our hearts sets us free. So why are so many believers living with different levels of bondage and defeat? One of the greatest reasons is we have left our first love. Our prayer must be "Lord restore my passion for Jesus." He has provided overwhelming victory in His blood. The blood sets mankind free from all bondage. In the days to come we will see a radical return to the message of Christ's redemptive blood. One does not have to continue living in defeat however; it will require our dedication to overcome the strongholds. If we will dedicate ourselves again and resolve to obey we can start walking in lifelong victory.

One of the most important aspects of the Christian walk is learning how to quickly obey the voice of the Spirit. Never run from God, but to Him. God longs to help us not hurt us. God has promised to never leave us but to always be with us. Thus we are assured of overwhelming victory because the victorious One abides within us.

The word "obey" is one of the strongest words in human language for hearing. The true evidence that we have heard Christ is that we are obeying His voice. True faith is always evidenced by obedience, which is why the word in the New Testament that is usually translated "faith" also means "faithfulness." True faithfulness with our life is evidenced by obedience to one of the main mandates that the Lord gave to us in Matthew 6:33-34: **"But seek first His kingdom and His righteousness; and all these things**

**shall be added to you. Therefore do not be anxious for
tomorrow; for tomorrow will care for itself."**

Many Christians seem to be as mixed-up as a termite
in a yo-yo. God is not the author of confusion. It is sad
to say that many Saints have spent too much of their lives
in disorientation and defeat because they have not obeyed
the Word of God. It is as we seek first the desire of the
King and the advancing of His kingdom that we have clear
guidance.

One source of confusion is that many are stumbling in
the light of their own sparks, not in the revealed light of
God's Word. They have made vital decisions based on their
own desires, and other earthly, temporary matters rather
than seeking first the purposes of the kingdom. If we based
all of our decisions on the purposes of His kingdom first,
everything else would have been added to us. If our lives
had been based on this, we would have nothing to be anxious about, knowing who our Source and Protector is.

There is no greater freedom, no greater peace, than that

which is the result of living our lives dedicated to the Lord in all things. We are being given another chance to do this now. Do not let this year pass like the others. Now is the time to walk in peace and freedom.

SOW YOUR SEED

Out my back door in the beautiful Blue Ridge Mountains of North Carolina is a huge apple orchard covering several hundred acres. It is a joy to watch the trees bud, bloom and bear delicious fruit. All this is the result of one single man with a big dream. Johnny Appleseed came through our region in Moravian Falls using the apple to preach the gospel. He used to say "You can count the seeds in an apple, but you can't count the apples in a seed." This whole region of the state is now covered in apple trees that supposedly originated from this evangelist who preached here more than 200 years ago.

What way is the Lord leading you to sow seeds for a harvest? Do not miss your opportunity. We are promised in both the Old and New Testaments, that we should have such an overflow that we are a major blessing to all who are in need. That's what Paul prayed for in 2 Corinthians 9:6-8:

> Now this I say, "he who sows sparingly shall also reap sparingly; and he who sows bountifully shall also reap bountifully. Let each one do just as he has purposed in his heart; not grudgingly or under compulsion; for God loves a cheerful giver. And God is able to make all grace abound to you, that always having all sufficiency in everything, you may have an abundance for every good deed...."

This is a part of our Promised Land, having such abundance, so much more than we need, that it blesses and touches everyone around us. This is not just in money or material things, but in faith, hope, love, healing, etc.

This process begins with material things because, as the Lord Jesus said, we cannot be trusted with the true riches of the kingdom if we do not learn how to handle the earthly ones (See Luke 16:11).

Even so, His kingdom is not of this world, and neither are the true blessings of the Promised Land that we are seeking. They are something we are to walk in and demonstrate in this life, but they are not of this world

TOUGH TIMES

This coming year is going to be very difficult for all who are not abiding in the kingdom. The fear barometer is going to be rising a few more degrees because the earth is going to be groaning and travailing, and the lawless are going to become even more ruthless. People who are giving themselves over to darkness are going to be falling into increasing darkness. However, the glory of the Lord which is coming by the Spirit upon His people will also increase.

Many don't like to hear such things, considering them to be "negative prophecies" but they are biblical prophecies. The times will not even be very difficult for those who have built their houses on the Rock by hearing and obeying the words of the Lord.

The Holy Spirit is going to be moving in a very dramatic way this year. Those who are in harmony with Him will be having the greatest year of their life. We really are coming to the time of the fulfillment of Isaiah 60:1-5:

> *Arise, shine; for your light has come, and the glory of the LORD has risen upon you. For behold, darkness will cover the earth, and deep darkness the peoples; but the Lord will rise upon you, and His glory will appear upon you. And nations will come to your light, and kings to the brightness of your rising. Lift up your eyes round about, and see; they all gather together, they come to you. Your sons will come from afar, and your daughters will be carried in the arms. Then you will see and be radiant, and your heart will thrill and rejoice; because the abundance of the sea will be turned to you, the wealth of the nations will come to you. (What bible translation is this? List it In parenthesis if it's different than what you've been using).*

We see here that at the very time the "deep darkness" is coming upon the world, the glory of the Lord is coming upon His people. If we are building our lives on the kingdom which cannot be shaken, we will have nothing to fear from the things that are now coming upon the world. Rather, it will be a time for great rejoicing—the time when the glory of the Lord appears upon His people. We must always keep in mind this is the greatest treasure, the greatest possession we could ever have—the Lord with us. We are going to be experiencing the glory of the Lord this year in an increasing way in preparation for the glorious victories to come. Get ready! The Lord is preparing us for His purposes--the establishing of His kingdom. We will be growing in the opposite spirit and growing in increasing respect for authority.

SUBMIT TO AUTHORITY

A kingdom is the realm that is under the king's authority. To be trusted with authority in the Lord requires that one be under authority. There is a respect for authority, rules, and order that we must have or we will be a great danger to ourselves and others if we were to be given more authority. This flies in the face of the way that the world is going, and we can expect this contrast to increase.

Authority, discipline, and rules are not necessarily legalism, though they can cross that line. However, in preparation for leadership in the Lord, I have not met one person who carries significant spiritual authority who was not at some time subjected to either an extreme form of legalism or overly controlling authority. One of the great examples of this in scripture is King David. King Saul was the tool that God used to fashion David into a great king.

How did David react to the unjust, demonized authority in his life? David honored him to the end, refusing to lift his own hand against Saul, even when he was trying to kill David. David even rewarded the men who recovered Saul's body and gave him a proper burial. He then went to a completely unprecedented extreme and honored Saul's children. This was exactly opposite of kings in those times, who quickly slew the children of any rivals. But David was of a different spirit.

It was David's great respect for authority toward those who were "anointed of the Lord" that enabled the Lord to entrust him with such remarkable authority that he was even used to establish the throne that the King of Kings would sit upon. The Lord Jesus Himself would be affectionately called "the Son of David." Now consider these exhortations from Scripture concerning authority:

> *Let every person be in subjection to the governing authorities. For there is no authority except from God, and those which exist are established by God. Therefore he who resists authority has opposed the ordinance of God; and they who have opposed will receive condemnation upon themselves. For rulers are not a cause of fear for good behavior, but for evil. Do you want to have no fear of authority? Do what is good, and you will have praise from the same; for it is a minister of God to you for good. But if you do what is evil, be afraid; for it does not bear the sword for nothing; for it is a minister of God, an avenger who brings wrath upon the one who practices evil. Wherefore it is necessary to be in subjection, not only because of wrath, but also for conscience' sake. Because of this you also pay taxes,*

for rulers are servants of God, devoting themselves to this very thing. Render to all what is due them: tax to whom tax is due; custom to whom custom; fear to whom fear; honor to whom honor.

(ROMANS 13:1-7)

It is noteworthy that the highest authority in Paul's world at the time he wrote this was Nero, who was one of the most corrupt, evil, and demented of the Caesars. He eventually executed Paul. Nowhere does it say to only be in subjection to the most righteous, just, authority, but rather "all" authorities.

Many are disqualifying themselves from receiving more Godly authority because they disrespect bosses and civil authority in its many and diverse manifestations. Remember, it was because of David's high calling that he was subjected to such a great test with a cruel, demented king like Saul. If you want to walk in great authority, learn to pass this test.

There is an erosion of respect for authority taking place in our times. This will happen before the end of this age, and it will be the primary cause for "the great time of trouble" or "the great tribulation" (See Matthew 24:21). However, regardless of how outrageous governments or the authorities become, those who will be trusted with the authority of the coming kingdom must in every way treat them with dignity and respect. This is "the Saul test."

Do not speak evil of your leaders. Do not disrespect the police, mayors, governors, or any others in authority, and teach respect for them to your children, beginning with their teachers, principles, etc. This does not mean that we cannot disagree with their policies or actions, and in the cases of teachers this might include some of their teachings, but we must do it in the most respectful way possible. In I Timothy 2:1-2, we are given a more positive approach to authority:

> *First of all, then, I urge that entreaties and prayers, petitions and thanksgivings, be made on behalf of all men, for kings and all who are in authority, in order that we may lead a tranquil and quiet life in all godliness and dignity.*

Here Paul exhorts them to do this "first of all."

In contrast to the growing lawlessness, there is an emerging generation of spiritual leaders who will come forth in the opposite spirit. These are the ones who will preach the gospel of the kingdom with power because they will have been found trustworthy to handle this authority.

It was the Gentile centurion who understood the nature of authority and how it came by being under authority. The Lord commended him as having greater faith than He had found in Israel (See Matthew 8:5-10). This is what we must understand if we are going to be trusted with the coming authority.

THE COMING ANARCHY

Before considering a few simple things that we can do to combat this growing lawlessness, let us take time to again consider what the Lord said about it in the following Scriptures:

> *Many will say to Me on that day, "Lord, Lord, did we not prophesy in Your name, and in Your name cast out*

demons, and in Your name perform many miracles?"
And then I will declare to them, "I never knew you;
depart from Me, you who practice lawlessness."

(MATTHEW 7:22-23)

The Son of Man will send forth His angels, and they
will gather out of His kingdom all stumbling blocks,
and those who commit lawlessness, and will cast them
into the furnace of fire; in that place there shall be
weeping and gnashing of teeth.

(MATTHEW 13:41-42)

Woe to you, scribes and Pharisees, hypocrites! For you
are like whitewashed tombs which on the outside ap-
pear beautiful, but inside they are full of dead men's
bones and all uncleanness. Even so you too outwardly
appear righteous to men, but inwardly you are full of
hypocrisy and lawlessness.

(MATTHEW 23:27-28)

"And because lawlessness is increased, most people's
love will grow cold. But the one who endures to the
end, he shall be saved."

(MATTHEW 24:12-13)

What must we do? First, we must understand that though we are not under the law, neither are we above it. We must submit ourselves to the Lord and respect His authority. We must teach our children to do the same. If we do not teach our children to respect authority, we are not equipping them for what will probably be the greatest battle they will have to face in these times. Remember why Abraham, the "father of faith" was chosen by God?

> *For I have chosen him, in order that he may command his children and his household after him to keep the way of the Lord by doing righteousness and justice; in order that the Lord may bring upon Abraham what He has spoken about him.*

> (Genesis 18:19)

The Lord said that He had chosen Abraham so that he would **"Command his children . . . after him to keep the way of the Lord…."** The very right of parents to exercise authority over their children is under increasing attack in these times. In this we must prevail for the sake of our children. However, it is essential that this be done in love, and not frustration, anger, impatience, etc. If we do not discipline with the fruit of the Spirit, it will be counterproductive and incite even further rebellion.

We must also understand that sin is lawlessness, and impurity leads to lawlessness. However, like faith, lawlessness usually begins with a seed, which is then watered and cultivated, bringing forth sin. According to 1 John 3:3-4 impurity and lawlessness are bound together **"And everyone who has this hope fixed on Him purifies himself, just as He is pure. Everyone who practices sin also practices lawlessness; and sin is lawlessness."**

It was Achan's lawless spirit and direct rebellion to Joshua and to God that had to be removed from the camp lest it spread. Achan's rebellion led to a dramatic death for himself and his whole family (See Joshua 7:20-26). Again we see the connection between sin and lawlessness, but Paul also provides the solution in Romans 6:19-23:

> *I am speaking in human terms because of the weakness of your flesh. For just as you presented your members*

as slaves to impurity and to lawlessness, resulting in further lawlessness, so now present your members as slaves to righteousness, resulting in sanctification. For when you were slaves of sin, you were free in regard to righteousness. Therefore what benefit were you then deriving from the things of which you are now ashamed? For the outcome of those things is death. But now having been freed from sin and enslaved to God, you derive your benefit, resulting in sanctification, and the outcome, eternal life. For the wages of sin is death, but the free gift of God is eternal life in Christ Jesus our Lord.

LOVE, NOT LEGALISM

Finally, consider how we can comply with the exhortation of Romans 13:8-14, which follows Paul's exhortation to honor those who are in positions of authority:

Owe nothing to anyone except to love one another; for he who loves his neighbor has fulfilled the law. For this, "You shall not commit adultery, You shall not murder, You shall not steal, You shall not covet," and if there is any other commandment, it is summed up in

this saying, "You shall love your neighbor as yourself."
Love does no wrong to a neighbor; love therefore is the
fulfillment of the law. And this do, knowing the time,
that it is already the hour for you to awaken from
sleep; for now salvation is nearer to us than when we
believed. The night is almost gone, and the day is at
hand. Let us therefore lay aside the deeds of darkness
and put on the armor of light. Let us behave properly
as in the day, not in carousing and drunkenness, not
in sexual promiscuity and sensuality, not in strife and
jealousy. But put on the Lord Jesus Christ, and make
no provision for the flesh in regard to its lusts.

Again, God's answer to lawlessness and rebellion is not legalism, but love. If we are growing in love for God and for others, it will be our desire to keep our hearts pure for them. Love is the fulfillment of the law, and it should be what motivates us to teach our children and to respect authority.

Do not waste the trials that come to you in many forms—in the church or in non-church relationships such as on your job, family, civil governments, etc. Like David, resolve to honor all who are in authority, and do not let bitterness or rejection find a place in your heart.

THE
CANDLE

*part*5

Preparations for Receiving Revelatory Light

Once, while waiting upon the Lord, I was ushered into a powerful prophetic encounter. I was surrounded by numerous magnificent heavenly messengers who quickly escorted me upward into the heavenly realm in front of a massive door.

I was stunned with its strength and beauty. This outstanding door was compelling and alluring in the noblest fashion. Intuitively I was aware that behind this door were divine treasures and wisdom beyond my ability to grasp. Written across the entrance in bold letters of living fire were two words "Spirit" and "Truth." The colors contained in these flames were beautiful beyond description. I was overwhelmed with the pull I sensed within my soul. I longed to behold what was beyond the door.

My heart pounded so hard each beat shook my body. I knew I was experiencing a moment of great opportunity and that something amazing was about to be revealed. I was simultaneously experiencing two opposite feelings: overwhelming anticipation along with holy fear and awe. The heavenly hosts who escorted me radiated tremendous might and power; however they were also exceptionally gentle and gracious. Their presence comforted and reassured me.

In this place of awe I couldn't muster the courage to ask; *Who has the key to such a significant door?* Even though I did not speak, one of the heavenly hosts answered in a reassuring tone. "The only key to this door is your deep desire to walk in Truth." When he said the word "Truth" I trembled knowing that this was much more than mere head knowledge. He was speaking about divine Truth.

The tone of his voice increased my deep desire to enter

the room. He continued "To the truly hungry this door is always open and accessible." A deep sense of assurance and hope washed over me. Jesus' promise in Matthew 5:6 rang in my heart. **"Blessed *are* those who hunger and thirst for righteousness, For they shall be filled."** I could hardly wait for the angel's next statement. Again his powerful yet reassuring voice instructed me "Extend your hand and touch the door." I touched the handle and was stunned when the door quickly swung open.

We can all be confident the Spirit of Truth is willing to aid us on our quest for Light and Truth. In 2 Samuel 22:29 we discover this tremendous promise: **"For You art my lamp, O LORD: and the LORD will lighten my darkness."** The Spirit of God will release the much-needed revelatory light if we are willing to seek Him while He may be found (See Jeremiah 29:12). We are in a season of revealed Truth. You have been given blessed and highly favored eyes and ears, which are able to comprehend this important truth (See Matthew 13:16).

ENTERING IN

Following angelic instructions I stepped inside. I was more than surprised. I had expected to be blinded by brilliant, blazing heavenly light, yet the room appeared almost completely dark. A small, flickering candle cast the faint light.

I intuitively knew that there was much more than what I could see with my natural eyes. In spite of the dim atmosphere, this room contained objects of immense worth--wisdom and knowledge on a level not yet discovered by mankind. Knowing this only intensified my desire to discover them. I was greatly encouraged by the promise in Proverbs 25:2 **"It is the glory of God to conceal a matter and the honor of kings to search it out."** It was my desire to search out this matter.

HUNGRY FOR TRUTH

God has given great, powerful promises to those who are spiritually hungry and thirsty. God promises to pour out His Spirit like floods of water in Isaiah 44:3-4.

> *For I will pour water on him who is thirsty, And floods on the dry ground; I will pour My Spirit on your descendants, And My blessing on your offspring; They will spring up among the grass Like willows by the watercourses.*

Our heart's cry must be that of Psalms 42:1-2 **"As the deer pants for the water brooks, So pants my soul for You, O God"** and Psalms 63:1-3, **"O God, You are my God; Early will I seek You; My soul thirsts for You; My flesh longs for You In a dry and thirsty land where there is no water."** We too must hunger and thirst for God. Ask now for an intensified hunger for Him.

THE CANDLEHOLDER

My heart was overcome with divine hunger. I longed for the light! I knew I would need a great deal more light to reveal the hidden treasures. In His light we will see light.

The candle was in a beautiful candleholder fashioned

from what appeared to be the purest gold. Although the flickering flame was small it was the outstanding brilliance of the candlestick that drew my attention. It was strong yet graceful and beautiful beyond description. It appeared to be made of pure gold. Suddenly I was aware of the Lord's presence. It seemed the more I focused upon the candlestick's beauty the more the room filled with His presence.

The whole atmosphere of the room was alive with Christ's presence and I desired to see Him more than any treasure hidden there. It is in Him that all the wisdom and treasures of God dwell (See Colossians 2:3).

My heart trembled with awe and anticipation at His presence. It was as if even the air became electrified with expectation. The awareness of Christ Jesus and His Majesty was breathtaking; it was wonderful and terrifying. Even the heavenly messengers were awed and astonished by the Lord's presence. Words cannot express the level of awe and reverence these angels have for the Lord. Their reaction only amplified the holy fear that gripped my heart.

Get ready! We are about to behold the Lord's majesty and might in such a way that will shock us. A totally different type of respect is coming in these days for Christ the King. We too will fall on our faces like John on the isle of Patmos when he encountered the risen Redeemer (See Revelation 1:10-18).

The holy reverential fear of the Lord was so strong I was afraid to breath. I was torn between two desires. I wanted to fall back into the shadows and hide yet at the same time I wanted the room to continue to flood with His holy presence.

I wanted to hide because of the contamination of my heart. In His presence I was keenly aware of the weakness and wickedness of my heart. In this moment I was conscious of the overwhelming grace of God toward us. Despite the fact that our sins are dreadful, through Christ's blood we become as white as snow (See Isaiah 1:18).

CONSIDER HIM

In Hebrews 12:3 we are instructed to "Consider Him ...." — Christ the Redeemer. For without Him we can accomplish nothing. It is the quest and goal to lift Him ever higher for all to see because He alone is all together lovely. As we lift Him up He draws all men unto Himself.

I love to study Hebrews chapter eleven uncovering the great exploits of men and women of outstanding faith. These people truly helped to advance God's kingdom. Our spirits are lifted higher as we reflect upon the great victories of the impressive roll call of faith's heroes and our expectation is heightened as we ponder these people. We do well to look deep into the life and ministry of these precious saints of old, but expect God to do even more in our day.

We must never forget that the greatest days of the church are ahead of us, we are to accomplish greater deeds than these spoken of in Hebrews. The Kingdom of God is about advancement and expansion. He has a mighty plan and awesome purpose for each of us. Never settle for less than God has promised to release for you. However our greatest quest is to behold the Lord in His glory, the main message is still to Consider Him. While our glance can rest upon these great heroes of faith our gaze must remain constantly affixed to the King of Kings. Yes, in all things we must consider Him. All our thoughts must lead to Him. So, no matter what the theme or text we are studying, we are really considering Jesus.

As we consider Jesus, we discover that truly He is altogether lovely. Great grace and anointing is upon the study of the Song of Songs in our day. The Holy Spirit has released much light upon the beauty of the Lord in this awe-inspiring passage of Scripture.

> *His legs are pillars of marble set on bases of fine gold. His countenance is like Lebanon, excellent as the cedars. His mouth is most sweet. Yes, he is altogether lovely. This is my beloved, and this is my friend, O daughters of Jerusalem!*
>
> (SONG OF SONGS 5:15–16)

Jesus alone is the fairest of ten thousand. He is the bright and Morning Star. He is the beautiful lily of the valley. Oh, how can we help but consider Him?

If we will take the time to study the book of Colossians we will discover much about the person, the power, and the position of Christ Jesus. In Colossians 1:15 we are told that Jesus is the image of the invisible God and the first-born of all creation. It is in Him that the fullness of the Godhead dwells.

Colossians 2:9–10 states **"For in Him dwells all the fullness of the Godhead bodily; and you are complete in Him, who is the head of all principality and power."** In Colossians 1:16–17 we discover that all things were created by Him and through Him, and that it is in Him all things continue to exist! Truly, God has highly exalted Jesus and given Him a name above every name. How can we not consider Him?

GIVING GLORY TO WHOM GLORY IS DUE!

Today when we observe God's mighty power demonstrated through a person we too must remember that behind it all is the Lord of Glory. We should never forget that it is God who works in us both to will and to do of His good pleasure (See Philippians 2:13). This is an overwhelming thought, that we can live our life so that it brings God pleasure. This must be the highest goal. We discover in Luke 12:32 that one of the things that brings Father God good pleasure is giving us the Kingdom, releasing to us divine authority.

As we keep this in mind, our appreciation for God's power moving in the life of others is heightened. It is wonderful to know that God chooses ordinary people and gives them an astounding anointing in order for them to accomplish the task He has assigned (See 1 Corinthians 1:26). The Scriptures declare concerning believers **"We have this treasure in jars of clay to show that this all-surpassing**

power is from God and not from us" (2 Corinthians 4:7). Truly God uses the ordinary to do extraordinary things so that when all is said and done He alone receives the glory due His name.

In the very near future we will see meetings where great displays of God's Spirit will accomplish overwhelming things and no one will go away speaking about the guest minister, but rather the whole focus will be upon the Lord of Glory.

I am convinced that God would do many more miracles if He would get the glory for them. This is something we must be very careful about — that we are always quick to give the glory to God for all that is accomplished in any of our ministry meetings.

In another powerful prophetic visitation I was told that the highest form of treason and the deepest betrayal was to take the gifts that God has released to win others to Christ and use these gifts and anointings to draw people to ourselves.

The Holy Spirit is on a mission — a mission to continually glorify the Lamb of God. He is drawing us to consider Jesus in all things, to fix our eyes on Him, knowing that as we look to Jesus we will become like Him. **"But we all, with unveiled face, beholding as in a mirror the glory of the Lord, are being transformed into the same image from glory to glory, just as by the Spirit of the Lord"** (2 Corinthians 3:18).

As we seek to behold Jesus in all His beauty, we will be changed to become more and more like Him. God desires to use us to become radical reflections of His glory, thus shining bright in a sin-darkened world. We must choose to allow the impartation of His life to become a sweet-smelling fragrance in our lives.

May it be stated of us like the early disciples that it is evident that we have been with Jesus. May the testimony of our lives be like that of Paul **"For me to live is Christ…."** May we never fail nor tire of lifting up the Son of God in order that He may continue to draw all men unto Himself.

Now let's return to the room with the candle. In the King's presence I longed to more clearly see His countenance. **"In the light of the King's face is life..."** (Proverbs 16:15). Knowing that Jesus sought to reveal many things to me I asked for strength to stand. Suddenly I felt His reassuring peace comforting my heart.

My voice trembled as I found the courage to ask "Lord what is this small candle?" He replied in the gentlest confirming tone "That is your spirit being awakened by My words." At His statement my heart filled with the promise found in Proverbs 20:27. **"The spirit of man is the candle of the Lord, searching all the inward parts of his being."** While I was thinking about this verse He said "Yes, it is true; I long to give more revelation to My people."

We are in the season of Truth; truly God will release His insights if we seek Him. In Psalms 18:28 we read these encouraging words: **"For you will light my candle; the Lord my God will enlighten my darkness."**

At the mere sound of His voice the flame began to vibrate. It grew stronger and stronger. I was amazed that the sound of His voice caused the flame to increase in power. As the room grew brighter and brighter so did my heart. It seemed to expand with each deposit. As the desire to see more increased in me, the Lord continued to speak concerning His Kingdom. With each word from His lips the room increased in light and brilliance. I was sadly and keenly aware of how little I knew concerning the King and His kingdom.

Worthy is the Lamb to receive all glory and honor. Here are some scriptures that pertain to this light. Psalms 36:9 **"For with You is the fountain of life: in Your light shall we see light."** Truly it is in His Light we see Light. Again in Psalms 18:28 **"For You light my lamp, The Lord my God illumines my darkness."** My heart began to cry out for more wisdom and understanding. We must have fresh revelation to accomplish what God is setting before our generation.

In the prophetic promise found in Isaiah 58:6-11 we discover awesome promises of light and health and overflowing provisions if we fully follow God's plans.

> *Is not this the fast that I have chosen? To loose the bands of wickedness, to undo the heavy burdens, and to let the oppressed go free, and that you break every yoke? Is it not to deal your bread to the hungry, and that you bring the poor that are cast out to your house? When you see the naked, that you cover him; and that you hide not yourself from your own flesh? Then shall your light break forth as the morning, and your health shall spring forth speedily; and your righteousness shall go before you; the glory of the Lord shall be your reward.*

As the Lord spoke again the small flame's radiance greatly increased. At the sound of His voice the entire room seemed to quiver and tremble--not in fear but rather in anticipation and expectation. In Psalms 29:8 we discover this truth: **"The voice of the Lord shakes the wilderness...."**

Christ continued to speak affirmingly. "The more you respond to My revelation the brighter your candle burns."

Even the instructions caused the flame to become noticeably brighter. With more light came more desire for light. The brighter the light the deeper grew my hunger for more. **"In Him was life, and the life was the light of men…"** (John 1:4).

In this incredible atmosphere I felt something deep within me arising, it was an excruciating hunger on a level I had never dreamed possible. The desire was like nothing I had ever experience before. It was a hunger for His Word and understanding. My heart cried out Psalms 43:3 **"O send out Your light and Your truth, let them lead me."**

Immediately I was more painfully and deeply aware of how little I truly know about His Majesty. It is one thing to know scripture in our head and a completely different thing to understanding divine Truth in our heart.

As we walk in His light we will see light. As He awakens our heart we will realize our desperate need for Him. A profound hunger arose within me. A deep love leaped within my heart. I cried out in desperation for more understanding. "Open my eyes to behold wonderful things from Your word. Open my ears to hear; open my eyes to see."

The cry of our heart is found in Ephesians 1:17-18 **"Open the eyes of my heart flooding it with revelatory truth giving me understanding of all you are saying to me.**

With each deposit of truth my hunger increased and the room became ever brighter. The shadows had been driven out and the room was radiant with the Glory of Christ. Soon I saw that this room was completely filled with awesome treasures of knowledge and wisdom, understanding and counsel but they must be accessed through the door of Spirit and Truth. These were not treasures such as gold and jewels, but true riches—the counsel of God, the wisdom of the Word of God. The mind of man cannot receive these treasures they must come through the revelation of the Spirit of Truth (See 1 Corinthians 2:9-14).

You Have a Candle Too

Each of us has been entrusted with a candle; we must respond to the Holy Spirit and permit Him to enlarge our flame. The candle is set aflame by Heaven's fire. In Job 29:3 we discover an awesome promise of walking in victory even in dangerously dark days: **"When his candle shined upon my head, and when by His light I walked through darkness."**

God's plan is for believers to walk courageously in the light, not stumble in the darkness. In Genesis 1:3 we discover God's heart. God said **"Let there be light: and there was light."** 1^John 1:5 tells us **"God is Light and in Him is no darkness at all."** We are called to be children of Light. We are to walk in the Light as He is in the Light, knowing that in Him is no darkness at all (See John 8:12). As followers of Christ each of us is called and commissioned to be children of the light. This is accomplished only as we walk directed by the Word of God. God's Word is the true lamp to our feet and a bright light to our path (See Psalms 119:105).

By believing and obeying, this much needed light releases true wisdom for our walk (See Psalms 119:130). Thus we are equipped to walk boldly and filled with divine confidence knowing that God has more power to direct us than the devil does to deceive us. The Word of God must be in our heart not just our head; we must be doers of the word and not just those who are content to hear. We are warned that this leads us into the deepest deception (See James 1:22). The Word of God is a powerful weapon in our spiritual warfare; it is the sword of the Spirit.

In a prophetic encounter the Spirit of God spoke these very encouraging words to me: "The people of God are about to believe what they know." This is extremely exciting news. We know quite a bit in our head, but seem to obey little in our heart. Now is the time to hear and heed the spoken Word as well as study the written Word and cry out for holy hunger and a brighter flame from the Lord.

THE LIVING ROD

A Heavenly Encounter

For months I have been seeking the Lord, asking Him for an increase in anointing, and for the much-needed authority in the days we are facing. Knowing we must have a powerful breakthrough (to go where God is calling us to go), and driven by my intense holy hunger, I had been asking for such an encounter. Consequently, in this atmosphere, I was expecting a precious grace gift.

I was swept into an extremely compelling prophetic encounter, without warning, when I was quietly waiting upon the Lord. I was completely overtaken by the most beautiful, breathtaking cloud. It appeared to be alive--shimmering with bright colors of gold and silver. Both alluring and alarming, the light was pure and piercing--bright beyond anything seen on earth. I was gripped with awe and apprehension at the same moment.

I fell on my face, breathless in delight and awe, and was instructed by a firm but loving voice. "Stand to your feet."

Not sure if my legs would support my body, and trembling with excitement and expectation, I arose. Standing in a thick cloud of God's glory, I intuitively knew I was about to be given something from Heaven.

The same voice instructed me to extend my hands, palms up. When I did so, from the golden cloud, an object was placed into my hands. I was sincerely shocked. I was given a stick about seven feet long, which was the size of a baseball bat's handle. The stick did not appear special or attractive, but it was much like a pole used for mountain hiking. It seemed so simple; I was quite surprised and somewhat disappointed. I was expecting something much more regal to be given in such an atmosphere of glory.

IT IS "THE ROD"

I asked the Heavenly messenger who delivered the stick "What is this?" He replied with immense joy "It is THE ROD!" There was esteem and irrepressible excitement in his voice. He spoke of The Rod with immeasurable delight. The tone and respect with which he spoke concerning the gift, caused my heart to stir, and I realized I had seriously misunderstood the magnitude and significance of this gift.

The angel instructed me. "You are to treasure this rod by placing it before the Lord, and releasing it back to Him." Now aware of its intense value, I deeply desired to guard The Rod--to protect it at all cost. I tightened my grip. Instantaneously I was standing in the presence of God's glory!

While everything within me longed to cling to the precious instrument, I was torn. Realizing the answer to my prayers and my longing for increased authority were now resting in my hands, and knowing what I held in my hand to be extremely precious, I also understood it was a gift and not mine. I knew I must obey the instructions of the Heavenly messenger. I must release The Rod.

I placed The Rod before the Presence of God's glory; I was filled with a wonderful sense of satisfaction. Amazingly, I realized that what I thought would be great loss, was now great gain. My heart leaped, knowing I had done the right thing. Words could not describe the tremendous joy that overflowed within me, as I heard words spoken from the midst mist of the glory cloud "Well done. Extend your hands. Take THIS!"

Abruptly appearing out of the midst mist of the Glory, The Rod was amazingly transformed. Standing upright (vertical), it was alive with Heaven's presence. It was living; pulsating with mighty, divine power!

As instructed, I took The Rod in my hands and as I did so, it was filled with buds, blooms and fruit! They appeared as the most precious jewels. Each bud was extremely beautiful. Blooms filled the entire place with an awesome aroma, and I was amazed at their precious fragrance. The fruit was abundant; beautiful beyond words. I was taken aback by the radical release of authority and power upon The Rod. It was truly something from another world. All this occurred in a moment's time and intuitively, I knew it was the harvest of the ages!

The Spirit of God is saying "If we will truly lay our ministries before Him, He will release evidence of true inward life, resulting in lasting fruit." The account of Aaron's rod is found in Numbers 17:8.

THE ANGELS OF AWAKING ARE RELEASED

Standing there in the presence of God's Glory, and beholding the Living Rod filled with its blooms and fruit, my nostrils filled with the sweetest smell. The fragrances were remarkable. When I asked "What flower is releasing such a wonderful aroma?" a reassuring voice from the Glory said "You smell the blooms of the Almond Tree!" At that declaration, my spirit began to tremble with expectation and anticipation. I felt overcome with the spirit of hope and shook with the sensation of sheer exhilaration. I asked "Lord what are these feelings?" He replied "I have released the Angels of Awakening."

At His declaration, the entire Heavens shook with a shutter of excitement. I could hear Heaven's hosts shouting with jubilation "On earth as it is in Heaven!" Again with even more power, they lifted their voices "On earth as it is in Heaven!" Their shouts rang out throughout the realms of glory! Soon we, on earth, will join their cry "On earth as it is in Heaven!" The gifts and anointing that God places upon our life are to establish the kingdom of God.

THE LIVING ROD RELEASES EVIDENCE

Aaron's rod bore evidence of God's approval and anointing. Suddenly in the night season, God was maturing Aaron's rod; making it ready to be revealed in the morning. Remember, weeping lasts a night, but joy comes in the morning (See Psalms 30:5). Never forget God begins His new day with the evening. Notice in Genesis 1:5 **"The evening and the morning were the first day."** Again in Genesis 1:8 **"The evening and the morning were the second day."** In Genesis 1:13 **"The evening and the morning were the third day."** So we see, God starts His new day with evening, not morning.

Get ready! During the dark nights, God is preparing to start His new day and your new day. You will awaken to a new dawn.

GOALS OF GRACE

part 6

As believers we are instructed to live our daily lives with true goals, aims, and divine purpose. We cannot achieve this unless we walk in God's grace.

God is not looking for strong people to help Him accomplish His work. The truth is that the Lord is looking for people who are weak enough to be used. We must remember that His strength is made perfect in our weakness (See 2 Corinthians 12:9). The key to experiencing supernatural liberating strength is personal weakness. Now let me make it clear that I am not speaking about weak character, or biblical knowledge. I am talking about a people who have come to the place where they have lost confidence in their fleshly power to accomplish the work of the

Spirit. It is at this point we become strong and "graced" to accomplish things for the true advancing of God's glorious kingdom.

This truth is clearly displayed in the story found in Psalm 107:23–28 of the strong, seaworthy sailors who made their living upon the high seas. However, one day the Lord raised up a stormy wind that blew away all their self confidence. They found themselves at their wit's end and they cried out for the Lord's grace and help. Though they were skilled and experienced, the winds and waves of the sea convinced them of their dependence upon God. Have you encountered the winds of change in your life? If not, you can be confident they are on their way.

Christ Jesus declares **"Without Me you can accomplish nothing!"** (John 15:5). This word "nothing" means: "completely, totally nothing." It truly means less than nothing. Ours is a life of joy when we come to the place where we understand that it must be the work of the Spirit to advance the kingdom of God.

Absolutely nothing you have ever done, nothing you could ever accomplish, will match the unparalleled joy of letting Jesus live His life through you. God has exactly fitted for each of us a unique walk of grace. As we yield our wills and ways to the Holy Spirit's control, we begin to experience this walk of grace. In this arena, you will experience the abundant grace that enables you to accomplish all that God has assigned you to do.

This deposit of grace is what makes the fire of passion burn so brightly in new believers over the things God is doing in their life. Their happiness and excitement is contagious. Their entire life is ablaze with God's love. As pastor, I was able to teach a new converts' class and my heart was always blessed by that joy. It is this grace that causes the light of contentment to dance in the eyes of mature believers who have learned the secret of walking in grace. Our life should testify to the ability of God's awesome grace to use us to accomplish great and mighty things for God's glory.

You cannot separate your daily actions from a grace-filled life. We are saved by grace, and we are kept by God's awesome grace. The Body of Christ seems to understand much concerning the grace of God touching an unbeliever's life, and bringing that person into a place of salvation. However, we lack true understanding concerning God's ability of grace to operate in the believers' daily lives, thereby bringing them into a place of true effectiveness and fruitfulness. Grace does not just change your mind. It has a transforming effect upon your life. Grace is a powerful motivator provoking us to reach higher and accomplish more for Christ and His kingdom.

ESSENTIAL INGREDIENTS FOR GRACE

The Apostle Paul stated in 1 Corinthians 15:10 **"But by the grace of God I am what I am, and His grace toward me was not in vain; but I labored more abundantly than they all, yet not I, but the grace of God which was with me."** Paul declared that the grace of God was not wasted upon his life, but he labored more because of the active grace in his life. Though all we are and all we do are because of God's grace, we are still called to labor abundantly to advance God's kingdom. One of the great paradoxes of the Christian life is that it is only by and through grace that we accomplish anything, yet God expects us to labor diligently in His service. Charles Spurgeon once said *"Faith goes up the stairs that love has built and looks out the window which hope has opened."*

Just as diligent labor is required to extract all of the grace that God has given us; humility is required to obtain grace. **"All of you, clothe yourselves with humility toward one another, because, 'God opposes the proud, but gives grace to the humble' "** (1 Peter 5:5). Grace is promised to the humble. A great saint of years by gone, Walter Buettler, made this observation — *"The moment humility announces herself she is already on her way out the door."* If we would be truly humble, and careful not to usurp God's glory, always giving Him praise for what He is doing, I am sure we would receive more grace. The Lord warned me once that the highest form of treason was to take the gifts and graces He has given leadership to win and woo the Bride to Himself, and then use these gifts and graces to win the Bride to ourselves.

May each heart embrace the promise given in Psalms 84:11 **"For the Lord God is a sun and shield; the Lord will give grace and glory."** In this passage we see the true key to advancing God's kingdom. It is by God's gift of grace that we are able to behold the glory. Any good thing ever accomplished by mankind is the direct result of the anointing and impartation of God's grace. May we walk a grace-filled life in order to see the glory of God fill the earth.

Grace is an open door which bids us to draw nearer to God. In Proverbs 8:17, 21 God declares **"I love those who love Me, and those who seek Me diligently will find Me ...That I may cause those who love me to inherit wealth, that I may fill their treasuries."** Now this is an awesome promise and powerful incentive, finding God and having Him bless us with overflowing treasures. We must never forget that God has great plans for His people. Hear His promise stated in Jeremiah 29:11 **"For I know the thoughts that I think toward you, saith the Lord, thoughts of peace, and not of evil, to give you an expected end."** It is time to open our hearts wide to God's grace and experience the good plans He has for each of us.

WAITING UPON GOD

The Lord desires to change us. He seeks to bring us up into His purpose. He waits for us to reach out to Him and knock on the door of His heart. Just as Esther had to approach her husband's throne, we too must prepare ourselves to approach God's throne. He, too, has extended His scepter. Now is the time grace has provided an open door in Heaven. Now it is time to approach the throne of God's grace to find favor and help during these days.

In Psalms 46:10 we are instructed to be still and know that God is God. Spending quiet time in the Lord's presence is necessary and carries great importance. It is as we wait upon Him that we are renewed in power and strength (See Isaiah 40:28–31). Each of us must find a special quiet place where we can shut out the cares of this world and get alone with God. Each day, we should come to our "set apart place" to worship, acknowledge His goodness and grace concerning us, and thank Him for His guidance and blessing upon our lives. Great grace is released when we truly enter His gates with thanksgiving and into His courts with praise. Make the time to praise the Lord and to bless His Holy Name!

As we take time to behold Him with an unveiled face, we are changed into ever increasing glory. In this place of quiet worship and prayerful reading of His Holy Word, there is a release of grace producing "Spirit and Life" which flows into our being to build our faith and provide the "enabling grace" for obedience. It is essential that we set apart time each day to be in His presence. Attending local church services are essential and not to be neglected, but this is no substitute for our devotional times alone with the Lord of Glory.

Being One with the Lord

Have you noticed in Luke 3:2 that the Word of God came to John the Baptist while he was alone in the wilderness? The programs of the "church" of that day were in full operation, yet John was called apart to be with the Lord alone. So also today, there are those who are spiritually hungry and seeking something more, who likewise are being called apart to be alone with the Lord for a time of preparation. As a result of his being alone with the Lord, John came into a oneness with the Lord that could not have been accomplished in any other way.

When John was asked who he was, his response testifies to this experience. He said **"I am the voice of one crying in the wilderness 'Make straight the way of the Lord,' as the prophet Isaiah said"** (John 1:23). Each one of us should come to the place where we also could make this statement — "I am the voice of One." There is an urgent need for this "voice" to cry out in the midst of the frustrations and perils of our present day. We live in a world that must have the grace and peace of God.

The need today is not new-fangled methodology, but rather a turning aside to stand in the manifest presence of the Lord to be prepared as "the voice of one crying in the wilderness" of our day. May it be stated of us, as it was of the disciples of old, that it is apparent that we have been with Jesus. This and only this will make the changes that must occur if we are to reach this hurting world with the message of God's redemptive, transforming grace.

Toward the end of his life, a popular minister was asked what he would do if he had his life to live over again. He said he had spent seven years in preparation for forty-five years of ministry. Instead, he would spend forty-five years in preparation for seven years of ministry. It is very important how we begin, but it is far more important how we end.

The Lord is seeking to bring us to the end of our abilities so we can tap into His ability. This requires that we recognize His presence and turn aside to stand before Him. Only then will we be enabled to become the expression of His voice — crying in the wilderness of our day.

part 7

GOD
VALUES YOUR
FRIENDSHIP!

The world we live in is extremely fast paced. Computers, iPods, cell phones, voice mail, e-mail, instant messaging, and other high tech gadgets seem to leave very little opportunity for really getting to know people and developing true, lasting friendships.

In our fast-paced world it is tragic to admit that many times it is the most important of these relationships, our companionship with Christ that suffers the most. The Spirit of God is calling each of us to turn aside from the cares and busyness of this world and come to Him for true companionship and friendship. Even in this frenzied, fast-paced world we can experience unparalleled peace and contentment if we walk in friendship with God. This vivid truth is portrayed in Luke 10:38-42 when Mary chose the most needful thing--to set at the feet of Christ allowing her thirsty soul to drink from the life- giving words flowing from His lips. Martha's motives were honorable and upright, her heart's desire was to do something helpful for Christ, however His deepest desire was to have communion and communication with someone.

Maintaining True FRIENDSHIP

As followers of Christ, even in the midst of a civilization that seems to shun true friendship, we must never lose sight of the fact that we have a true Friend in "high places." This true Friend is none other than the Son of God, Christ the Lord and He remains closer than a brother. We could have no higher privilege than to be known as a true friend of God.

The happiest people on earth are the ones who have surrendered control of their lives to the Spirit of God and entered into this friendship. Remember, a true friend is one

who is always there for you. You can confide the deepest secrets of your heart with a dear, trusted friend. God, too, will
share His secrets with His trusted Friends. Jesus promised
us in John 15:15: **"No longer do I call you servants, for a
servant does not know what his master is doing; but I
have called you friends, for all things that I heard from
My Father I have made known to you."** The songwriter of
old said it well. "What a friend we have in Jesus ..."!

Value And Worth

God highly values not only His friendship with you,
but you yourself. The Lord has ascribed to you great worth.
Countless numbers of Christians have never stopped to
ponder the great value that God has placed upon their
lives. It is almost overwhelming to consider the fact that
Almighty God has chosen you to become the eternal companion of His dear Son!

Can you imagine that with the entire universe under His
control and care, Father God actually delights and takes

pleasure in fellowshipping with you? Truly you are extremely special to God. Knowing this, you should never be plagued with thoughts of unworthiness or feeling that your life has no true meaning or purpose. Christ would have done all that He did in coming to earth and dying on the cross if you were the only one on earth that needed redemption. That is how special you are to God! Heaven places great worth and value upon you. You are incredibly special to God.

How do we ascertain what something is worth? What determines its value? The answer is: what someone is willing to pay for it. Think about it. God was willing to give Heaven's best — His own Son — to redeem you. Now that shows your true worth and reveals your eternal value. Don't ever allow the enemy to make you feel like you don't have any real worth.

The Creator of the entire universe desires that you be in His presence for all eternity. There is no need to suffer in despair and loneliness when Christ reaches out to each of us and offers true love and friendship.

Living With Purpose — Not Stardom

If we walk daily in friendship and union with Christ, the Scripture promises **"But if we walk in the light as He is in the light, we have fellowship with one another, and the blood of Jesus Christ His Son cleanses us from all sin"** (1 John 1:7). This is where our cleansing, contentment, and comradeship stem from — union with Christ. As we abide in Him, our life finds its purpose and pleasure.

The most confident people on the face of the earth are Christians who are totally yielded to the control of God's Spirit. Since we know that God has good plans for our lives we are called to live with a divine goal, aim, and purpose. **"See then that you walk circumspectly, not as fools but as wise, redeeming the time, because the days are evil. Therefore do not be unwise, but understand what the will of the Lord is"** (Ephesians 5:15–17). We should be living in a wise and worthy manner, which means following the plan for which God gave us life. To truly accomplish this we must be guided daily by the Holy Spirit. Then our lives will be fulfilled.

Now is the time for the history makers to take their place. The Spirit of Truth is erasing a huge lie that has paralyzed the body of Christ, which says God only uses the "superstar saint." Nothing could be farther from biblical truth. God uses ordinary people to accomplish extraordinary exploits. Remember, the promise of Isaiah 40:31 is for all who hope in the Lord: **"Those who hope in the Lord will renew their strength. They will soar on wings like eagles; they will run and not grow weary, they will walk and not be faint."**

THE RESULT OF FRIENDSHIP

The Spirit of God has chosen you to live during these important days in history. Each of us should strive to accomplish great things for God's glory. The greatest achievement we are called to is a continuing companionship and friendship with Christ. As we walk in this, we will become overcomers.

Our friendship with Christ helps prepare us for the harvest. The church must be equipped to handle the coming waves of people. The masses of people that are coming will be from every walk and every level of society. Nothing can qualify us for this gathering of the harvest more quickly than friendship with Christ. It is only as the world takes notice that we have been with Christ that our witness will ring true. This is what the leaders in Jerusalem said about Peter and John. **"When they saw the courage of Peter and John, and realized that they were unschooled, ordinary men, they were astonished and they took note that these men had been with Jesus"** (Acts 4:13). May the same be said about us; may the world see us as those who not only know about Christ, but know Him and are known by Him.

Defeating the Devil Through Christ's Sufficiency

part 8

Many years ago Dr. Billy Graham, in his *Decision* magazine, sent out a questionnaire to church leadership, as well as others, asking for a response to this intriguing question: "How do you handle temptation? How do you walk victoriously while dealing defeat to the devil?" After compiling responses for several months he would print what he felt was the very best answer.

I could hardly wait. I was sure some leading theologian would arrive at a stunning answer that would give great help to the body of Christ; advancing us in this area of spiritual warfare. Finally the day came when the issue arrived. Dr. Graham said that out of all the brilliant answers he had received from the many important leaders this was what he considered the very best response. My eyes quickly scanned for the award-winning answer. But just then in a footnote I noticed Dr. Graham added that the award-winning response came from a nine-year-old girl! I was shocked. Are you as eager to hear what she reported as I was? Well here it is: *"When I hear the devil knocking at my heart's door ...I just send Jesus to answer the door!"*

That is truly an awesome answer to the complicated questions arising from spiritual warfare. Our victory rests solely in the Victorious One — Christ Jesus. We must grasp the child-like faith in the little girl's simplistic answer.

Have you ever observed two children as they argued with one another "My daddy can whip your daddy"? This is how we must be in regard to spiritual conflict. We, too, must have total confidence in the ability of our Heavenly Father to handle anything that the enemy of our soul can bring our way, remembering the promise that no weapon formed against us can succeed (Isaiah 54:17). Over and over we are reminded in Scripture of the power and authority we have been given in Christ. Jesus said:

Behold! I have given you authority and power to trample upon serpents and scorpions, and physical and mental strength — ability over all the power that the enemy possesses: and nothing shall in any way harm you.

(LUKE 10:19, AMPLIFIED)

It is time to take the authority that God has given and stand against the foe. We are told in James 4:7 that if we will resist the devil he will flee. But first we are instructed to draw near to God, then we are prepared to better resist the devil. As we learn to live close to our glorious Lord, we will develop great confidence to declare His ability and willingness to overcome the enemy, no matter how he chooses to attack us.

What we need is to truly know God in order to be strong and prepared to accomplish great things. **"The people who know their God shall be strong, and carry out great exploits"** (Daniel 11:32). Understanding more about *Who* God is will better equip us to know *What* He has promised to do in and through us as we trust Him.

Paul states:

> *I have strength for all things in Christ who empowers*
> *me. I am ready for anything and equal to anything*
> *through Him who infuses inner strength into me: I*
> *am self-sufficient in Christ's sufficiency.*

(PHILIPPIANS 4:13, AMPLIFIED)

This must become the center of our focus as we face spiritual opposition, not the problem but the solution — the sufficiency of Christ.

THE WARRIOR KING

To help us get a better perspective of who Christ Jesus really is, we need to observe Him. The Scriptures declare **"My people perish for a lack of knowledge."** We lack a true knowledge of who Christ is in the aspect of *Warrior King.*

> *We know that Christ is gentle and mild, but when it*
> *comes to warfare against the rulers of darkness it is a*
> *different story. In the book of Revelation we see Jesus*
> *not as the sweet, perfect baby of Bethlehem, nor the*

suffering Savior dying upon Calvary's cruel cross, but as the Risen, Ruling, Reigning Redeemer clothed in absolute power and authority.

Now I saw heaven opened, and behold, a white horse. And He who sat on him was called Faithful and True, and in righteousness He judges and makes war. His eyes were like a flame of fire, and on His head were many crowns. He had a name written that no one knew except Himself. He was clothed with a robe dipped in blood, and His name is called The Word of God. And the armies in heaven, clothed in fine linen, white and clean, followed Him on white horses. Now out of His mouth goes a sharp sword, that with it He should strike the nations. And He Himself will rule them with a rod of iron. He Himself treads the winepress of the fierceness and wrath of Almighty God. And He has on His robe and on His thigh a name written: "KING OF KINGS AND LORD OF LORDS."

(Revelation 19:11–16)

We must remember that the Kingdom of Heaven suffers violence and the violent take it by force (See Matthew 11:12). As believers, this is not a time to be complacent. We must become much more aggressive in our stance against the powers of darkness. We must learn how to take the authority God has given to us to unlock heavenly treasures concerning our spiritual destiny. There are things in the heavens that we need to loose in order to have them on earth.

Our tongues are the keys that open Heaven's treasure chest. It was Peter's bold confession of who the Lord was that released the promise of power and helped launch him deeper into his destiny. We, too, must begin to make declarations. The Scriptures tell us that we are to decree a thing so that it can become established (See Job 22:28).

It is only as we stand strong in the Lord and in the power of His might that we can overcome the powers of darkness. God has promised that we are victorious because He is in us and we are in Him. Listen to these encouraging words found in 1^John 4:4 **"Little children, you are of God, you belong to Him and have already defeated and overcome them, the agents of the anti-Christ, because He who lives in you is mightier than he who is**

in the world" (Amplified). Though we may be only little children in the spiritual realm, because we are in Christ and He is in us, Jesus will defeat the enemy through us and cause him to flee.

One of the pictures the Bible paints for us of Jesus is that of Him being our "elder brother." When the hordes of the enemy confront us, when we have giants of opposition, we can let our "Big Brother" who is the Warrior King answer their taunting. He will win the victory — either for us or through us!

That little girl was right; when the devil is knocking at our door the best thing any of us can do is send Jesus to answer the door. Amen!

SEEING THE GOODNESS OF GOD

"I love them that love Me; and those that seek Me early shall find Me . . . . That I may cause them that love me to inherit substance; and I will fill their treasures" (Proverbs 8:17, 21).

God is good! This statement is without question absolutely true. However, I feel we have made the statement almost a meaningless cliché. In Nahum 1:7 we discover this awesome promise **"The Lord is good, a strength and stronghold in the day of trouble; He knows those who take refuge and trust in Him."**

The goodness of God does not rest in what is taking place in our lives or the situation we find ourselves in. God's goodness is brought into question many times because we think He is good only if things are going great, and our life is free from troubles and trials. But the goodness and faithfulness of God is a constant. He never changes in His love for us, no matter how our situations change.

At the conclusion of a recent meeting in the Northwest, I was ministering to a long line of people. One of these was a young man in his early twenties. When I looked into his eyes, I saw such anger and hurt, his first words to me were shocking. He said with a voice filled with hot anger--"I don't trust God!" Yet, though the hurt and anger were so strong, I knew that he was a true believer and a real Christian. I asked him "Why don't you trust the Lord?" In sobs and gasps he told me the story of his mother's sudden and tragic death. He had not been able to say good-bye. His heart was so heavy and wounded, to simply say to him "Well, you know God is good" seemed a bit empty.

So I took him in my arms and he clung to me weeping as I attempted to explain to him that truly God is good. I also explained to him that we do not have all the answers, in many things we see darkly like looking through a glass. His heart was helped as we talked about the promise that all things work together for good. Many have been misled by thinking this Scripture states that everything that happens will be good. No, God in His grace and tender mercy can cause all things to work together for good. My advice to him was to just keep his heart open and not grow bitter and cold toward the Lord but instead to draw even closer. Then I released this verse filled with hope into his heart **"But they that wait upon the Lord shall renew their strength…"** (Isaiah 40:31).

IT'S TIME TO WAIT

Our generation finds it extremely hard to wait--on any-thing. We want to maximize every moment. However, as believers we must acquire the discipline of spending time with the Lord. "Waiting upon the Lord" is a discipline that is either unknown or not valued by most Christians. Yet, once you have tasted the fruit of time spent waiting in the presence of the Lord, you can be satisfied with nothing less. You were created to abide in God's presence. Only in His presence does our longing heart find true peace and our life takes on richer more purposeful meaning.

The Lord is looking for those who know His presence and understand His ways. We will not be able to cultivate these abilities in our spiritual lives, unless we first learn to wait upon Him. This waiting on the Lord must be practiced each day if these qualities are to become a reality in our lives.

ENTER GOD'S WAITING ROOM

There are many aspects of waiting on the Lord. I am not talking about living a lonely secluded life. True "waiting" includes three steps. The first step has to do with a withdrawal from activity, along with a corresponding entering into a quietness and rest within our spirits. The second step is birthed within this newfound quietness, as we begin to actively wait *for* His manifest presence, or directive. **"Be still, and know that I am God; I will be exalted among the nations, I will be exalted in the earth!"** (Psalms 46:10). Something amazing occurs when we take time to sit at His feet, for it is really only from the position of sitting at Jesus' feet that we are able to know how to serve Him in a way pleasing to Him. In the story of Mary and Martha (See Luke 10:38–42), Martha's heart to serve Jesus is wonderful (how much this heart is needed today in the church), but Jesus' desire for each of us is that we would first wait for Him, and then knowing both His goodness and His desires go forth to serve Him.

A return to activity is the third step of waiting on the Lord. When the Lord responds to our waiting *for* Him and comes into our midst, we then begin to wait *upon*

Him — acknowledging His presence as being with us, and then cooperating with Him in whatever way He may lead or instruct. This third step cannot be done unless we have fulfilled the first and second steps.

Waiting on the Lord also includes a daily "continuous waiting." The cultivation of His abiding presence in our daily lives has to do with the "poise" of our spirit being lifted toward Him in faith and expectancy, and then continually waiting on Him during our times of activity.

I am often asked "How can you be so busy, traveling hundreds of thousands of miles a year in ministry and still maintain close fellowship with Christ?" The answer is that you can be shut in with God in the midst of activity! To be able to do this will take time. I have learned the secret of getting alone with God even in a crowd. The secret is to first learn to wait on the Lord in our secret closet. Then, I am able to carefully carry His presence with me into times of activity. In your spirit you can shut out the world and get alone with the Lord even in the midst of crowds. Learn to focus your mind upon the Lord. **"You will keep him in perfect peace, whose mind is stayed on You, because he trusts in You"** (Isaiah 26:3).

Fixing Our Minds on Christ

If we are going to keep our mind stayed upon Jesus, we must determine to wait upon the Lord, and to have His abiding presence in our lives. Next, we must set aside a time and a place for this purpose. Then, begin to wait upon the Lord. One of the best times is when you first awake in the mornings. Give that special time to the Lord, and ask Him to direct your every move during the entire day. Thank Him for all His goodness in your life. Just spend time loving on Him! When this is the first order of your day, your whole day will be much more productive.

We can do this as we begin to worship the Lord and meditate on Him. The fact of the Lord's presence being with us, as revealed in Jeremiah 23:24 will help us to do this: **"'Can anyone hide himself in secret places so I**

shall not see him?' says the Lord. 'Do I not fill heaven and earth?' says the Lord." Once the truth of this scripture really gets hold of us, we can assure ourselves that God is present, and that we are not alone.

The fact that His presence is with us when we wait upon Him causes a spiritual renewing process to take place in our lives, connecting us with God through faith, and then leading us into a conscious revelation of Him. When first beginning this practice, out minds and flesh will rebel, but persevering in waiting will pay off with His presence and your emerging sensitivity of things of the Spirit. You may not feel anything is happening at first, but this experience will grow gradually, and become your delight. The key is to not become discouraged and stop. You will eventually experience Him if you persist.

Our minds will be renewed as we wait upon Him, so that our mind is progressively brought closer to His mind, until **"We have the mind of Christ"** (1 Corinthians 2:16). As you learn to continually abide in His presence, you will no longer be **"Conformed to this world, but be transformed by the renewing of your mind"** (Romans 12:2). This transformation is worked in us as we take time to wait in His presence. Through this, we come to know the thought of God toward us, and are enabled to walk in His will and ways.

As we wait upon the Lord, the Spirit of Truth will renew our minds and reassure us concerning the goodness of God. This is what David did when he was in deep distress. When great defeat and discouragement surrounded David's life, he encouraged himself in the Lord. **"And David was greatly distressed ... but David encouraged himself in the Lord his God"** (1 Samuel 30:6). We too can cast our cares and troubles upon the Lord and He will release great grace.

Waiting on God is a discipline for which few are willing to pay the price in this day of activity and pressure. But those who have learned the secret of entering into His presence have found the pearl of great price. It is as we meditate upon the Lord that our hearts and minds are renewed. No matter what may come our way we will be confident that God is good and His mercy endures forever.

ABIDING
IN THE
ANOINTING

part 9

J esus Christ reveals the only authentic source of anointing and power in His words, in the John 15:1-7

I am the true vine, and my Father is the husbandman. Every branch in me that beareth not fruit he taketh away: and every branch that beareth fruit, he purgeth it, that it may bring forth more fruit. Now ye are clean through the word which I have spoken unto you. Abide in me, and I in you. As the branch cannot bear fruit of itself, except it abide in the vine; no more can ye, except ye abide in me. I am the vine, ye are the branches: He that abideth in me, and I in him, the same bringeth forth much fruit: for without me ye can do nothing. If a man abide not in me, he is cast forth as a branch, and is withered; and men gather them, and cast them into the fire, and they are burned. If ye abide in me,

and my words abide in you, ye shall ask what ye will,
and it shall be done unto you.

It is imperative that we cultivate abiding in His presence. This does not come easy, many will be the distractions as well as the attractions provided by the foe of your soul, attempting to prevent intimacy between us and the Lover of our soul. We must learn how to keep our mind and heart stayed upon the Lord (See Isaiah 26:3-4).

ABIDING IN JESUS IS ESSENTIAL TO BEARING FRUIT

The promise is very clear if we abide in Christ we will be fruitful. If we fail to abide in Jesus we become unfruitful and are in danger of being cast aside. Jesus reminds us very firmly "without HIM we can accomplish nothing. This word nothing is a strong word, it is the Greek work "oudeis" which means a zero with a vacuum in it. It means absolutely nothing. This word means total failure. That is what happens if we attempt to accomplish anything apart from total dependence on Christ. We can do nothing. However it is very encouraging to know that with Him and by Him we can accomplish anything.

God's Own Garden

In John 15, Jesus used the word "husbandman" to define His Father. Figurative: Jesus said "I am the true vine, and my father is the husbandman." He plants, cultivates, prunes and expects fruits from His church. The church is alluded to as "God's husbandry" by Paul in 1 Corinthians 3:9.

It is very important to grasp the term "husbandman." Let's examine some translations of this word. Paul used this same word to help describe the Body of Christ in 1 Corinthians 3:9 **"For we are laborers together with God: ye are God's husbandry, ye are God's building."** In this passage we discover ourselves being described as "God's own garden" or "God's tilled field."

Notice the term Jesus used to described Father God in John 15:1 **"I am the true Vine, and my Father is the**

Gardener." Again in the (RSV) we read **"I am the true vine, and my Father is the Vinedresser."** How wonderful to know that He will tend us with loving care. He will bring the right amount of sunshine and rain into our life. The Divine Gardner will always do for us and in us what will produce the most fruit through us.

One of the most important responsibilities of the Vinedresser is that of pruning to cut away useless branches that hinder true fruitfulness. The Greek word is "kathairo" which means - to cleanse of filth, impurity, etc. Also to prune trees and vines from useless shoots, metaphorically, to cleanse from guilt, to make amends, or to atone.

Jesus used almost the same word - which speaks of essentially the same action when He said "takes away." This word means lifting up the anchor of a ship so that it can sail away. God does this to the unproductive parts of our life that keep us from being able to bear good fruit; He prunes them and sends them away.

The word abide is a precious word: it deals with taking

up permanent residence. Many are the precious promises released to us if we abide in Jesus and let the Word of God abide in us. We have the promise of answered prayers. The Lord is answering the plea and prayer of His disciple found in Luke 11:1 **"Lord teach us to pray."** As we abide in Him we can ask and receive, it is the Father's good pleasure to give us the Kingdom (See Luke 12:32). It will produce great joy to see your prayers answered. (See John 16:24). God will answer our prayers and reveal to us great and mighty things of which we have no comprehension (See Jeremiah 33:3).

Abiding in God's Presence

Have you ever wondered just what qualifies one to go to the next level of anointing or just how God positions some in places of leadership? One explanation is found in Joshua's life. In Exodus 33:3 we are told of the manifested presence of God coming down into the Tabernacle in a cloudy pillar. One little statement stands out **"He stayed**

in the Tabernacle." Joshua would not leave God's presence. This is what qualified him to be the next leader of God's people. He so loved to be in arena of the anointing. The longing of his heart was to stay in God's presence.

Remember it is only the manifested presence of God that makes us unique. Moses pleaded with God saying **"God if your presence does not go with us we do not want to go."**

Let's review this conversation between Moses and God, recorded in Exodus 33:11-16:

> *Inside the tent the Lord spoke to Moses face to face, as a man speaks to his friend. Afterwards Moses would return to the camp, but the young man who assisted him, Joshua (son of Nun), stayed behind in the Tabernacle. Moses talked there with the Lord and said to him, "You have been telling me, 'Take these people to the Promised Land,' but you haven't told me whom you will send with me. You say you are my friend, and that I have found favor before you; please, if this is really so, guide me clearly along the way you want me to travel so that I will understand you and walk acceptably before you.*

For don't forget that this nation is your people." The Lord replied, "I myself will go with you and give you success." For Moses had said, "If you aren't going with us, don't let us move a step from this place. If you don't go with us, who will ever know that we have found favor with you, and that we are different from any other people upon the face of the earth?"

Many circumstances capture our attention from this passage of scripture. First, it is wonderful to know God longs to communicate with us. It is marvelous to know that God spoke to Moses face to face as a man speaks to his friends (See John 15:15). This knowledge should compel us to do all we can in order to be called a FRIEND of GOD. God shares His secrets with His friends.

Once I asked the Lord about a prophetic man, who at that time in his life was going though much controversy. The Lord said to me "He is MY FRIEND!" That was all I needed to know.

Second, we learn from this passage that God will give us clear directions as we seek His leadership. If we have the heart of Joshua longing to abide in the place of anointing, we too can be transformed. As we behold Christ Jesus we are transformed into His likeness.

OUR POSITION IN CHRIST JESUS

The Lord is speaking to the Body of Christ today from the first chapter of the book of Ephesians. It is very interesting to look over the little word "in." It is used over 25 times. As we ponder the use of this word we gain much needed assurance of our position in Christ. Also we much have confidence in the provisions of Christ. We would do well to study very closely the use of this little yet very important word "IN."

Notice just a few of these "in's" found in Ephesians 1:2-11:

> *Grace to you and peace from God our Father and the Lord Jesus Christ. Blessed be the God and Father of our Lord Jesus Christ, who has blessed us with every spiritual blessing* **in** *the heavenly places* **in** *Christ, just as He chose us* **in** *Him before the foundation of the*

world, that we should be holy and without blame before Him in love, having predestined us to adoption as sons by Jesus Christ to Himself, according to the good pleasure of His will, to the praise of the glory of His grace, by which He has made us accepted in the Beloved. **In** *Him we have redemption through His blood, the forgiveness of sins, according to the riches of His grace which He made to abound toward us in all wisdom and prudence, having made known to us the mystery of His will, according to His good pleasure which He purposed* **in** *Himself, that* **in** *the dispensation of the fullness of the times He might gather together* **in** *one all things in Christ, both which are in heaven and which are on earth—*in Him. **In** *Him also we have obtained an inheritance, being predestined according to the purpose of Him who works all things according to the counsel of His will..."*

(EMPHASIS MINE)

Only as we abide *in* HIM do we have true victory, because it is *in* Him we live and move and have our being. It is in HIM that we find all Wisdom and Knowledge. It is *in* HIM that the fullness of the Godhead dwells. May great grace be granted to each of us causing us to come to Christ and set at His feet, as did Mary, enabling us to do the one thing that is most needful, abide *in* His presence. Only then can we bear true fruit that will remain.

LONGING TO SEE GOD'S GLORY

The Spirit of the Lord is speaking exceptionally clear and powerful to the church. We must have our ears open to hear His voice. Revelation 3:22 says **"He who has an ear, let him hear what the Spirit says to the churches."**

START THINKING BIG

I was challenged by the Lord to attempt to exaggerate what He was about to do. My mind raced as I began to think about the definition of the word "exaggerate." The word will truly stir you and release excitement in your spirit. It is made up of two thoughts "to heap up" and "to carry forward." It means: *"to enlarge beyond bounds or pre-conceived truths; to overstate; to enlarge or increase beyond the normal."* I said "Oh Lord, give me a verse to back this up." Quickly He gave me these words **"Now to Him who is able to do exceedingly abundantly above all that we ask or think, according to the power that works in us"** (Ephesians 3:20).

So I want you to think big and expect big things from God. The Spirit of God is not bound by our lack and limitations. God is about to move us past our ability to comprehend. We must never try to limit God by what we understand. Hear the thundering voice of God as He boldly declares **"Behold, I am the Lord, the God of all flesh: is there anything too hard for Me?"** (Jeremiah 32:27). May our answer resound with this shout of confidence **"Ah Lord God! Behold, You have made the heavens and the earth by Your great power and outstretched arm. There is nothing too hard for You"** (Jeremiah 32:17).

These will be days when the church begins to see the supernatural manifested power of God active in our midst like never before. It is going to take the power of God to move this generation. God will release His power to reach this harvest (Acts 1:8). The mighty works of God are necessary to reach the masses of people. **"Then a great multitude followed Him, because they saw His signs which He performed on those who were diseased"** (John 6:2). Here we see this truth declared. Miracles manifest the glory of God and cause even followers of Christ to become even more steadfast in their faith. **"This beginning of signs Jesus did in Cana of Galilee, and manifested His glory; and His disciples believed in Him"** (John 2:11).

Notice what happened. Jesus' glory was manifested and even His disciples were drawn closer because they saw a miracle — the water being turned into the best wine. I think this miracle is also reflected in what the Spirit is doing today in the church. He's filling the water pots (us) to the brim with the water (the Word), and now the changing into the best wine is coming (anointing for these days).

GET READY TO SEE HIS GLORY

To empower and anoint the saints to win the world, the Lord will begin to manifest His glory. Listen to this promise in Habakkuk 2:14: **"For the earth shall be filled with the knowledge of the glory of the Lord, as the waters cover the sea."** The Lord has promised that the entire earth will be filled with the knowledge of God's glory. The word used here for glory is "kabowd" or "kobod" which speaks of the heavy, thick, concentrated presence of God — a presence that has substance. The word for knowledge is "yada" which means *"understanding, comprehension, perception, the acquired knowledge, or the discernment of something."* This is a powerful word which has a variety of very colorful meanings. One, it is the word for becoming one with, like a husband and wife in the act of intercourse. So we are about to get to know more intimately about the manifested Glory of God.

The church at the end of the age will be more glorious than it was at its beginning, even more glorious than the Jewish Temple of the Old Testament. In Haggai 2:7, 9 God promises **"'And I will fill this house with glory. ... The glory of this latter house will be greater than of the** former,' says the Lord of hosts. 'And in this place I will give peace,' says the Lord of hosts."

Look at the glory of the first house in 2 Chronicles 7:1–3:

> *When Solomon had finished praying, fire came down from heaven and consumed the burnt offering and the sacrifices; and the glory of the Lord filled the temple. And the priests could not enter the house of the Lord, because the glory of the Lord had filled the Lord's house. When all the children of Israel saw how the fire came down, and the glory of the Lord on the temple, they bowed their faces to the ground on the pavement, and worshiped and praised the Lord, saying: "For He is good, for His mercy endures forever."*

When the glory of God comes, no man will be able to stand up and minister. First Kings 8:11 shows us this: **"So that the priests could not stand to minister because of the cloud: for the glory of the Lord had filled the house of the Lord."** The Lord Himself by the Spirit will conduct the ministry.

Preparing for God's Glory

The glory of God will not only draw new believers into the kingdom, it will draw the saints closer to Jesus, and cause them to begin to prepare to meet their Bridegroom. The Lord Jesus will be presented with a beautiful, anointed "bride" as the Scripture teaches in Ephesians 5:26–27:

> *That He might sanctify and cleanse her with the washing of water by the word, that He might present her to Himself a glorious church, not having spot or wrinkle or any such thing, but that she should be holy and without blemish.*

The Lord will cleanse His church, removing the "spots" and applying "heat" and "pressure" to remove the wrinkles. Very soon now we will hear this statement spoken **"Who is this coming up from the wilderness, leaning upon her beloved?"** (Song of Solomon 8:5).

Yes, the church has been in a terrible wilderness, not sure who or where she was. Yet her Lover, the Lord Jesus, has come to her rescue and is bringing "her" up out of the

place of confusion. The world will no longer mock, saying "What is this?" but now "Who is this?" The end-time
church will be marked by a transforming beauty and holiness which will be irresistible. Listen to these words of love
as Christ prophetically sets forth the condition the church
will be in. **"You are all fair, my love, and there is no spot
in you"** (Song of Solomon 4:7).

The Church Must Become Pure

If we are to experience true intimacy and fellowship
with Christ, we must be pure. The Psalmist asked **"Who
may ascend into the hill of the Lord? And who may
stand in His holy place? He who has clean hands and a
pure heart, who has not lifted up his soul to falsehood"**
(Psalm 24:3–4). Only the pure in heart will gaze on and
behold the Lord. Christ reminds us **"Blessed are the pure
in heart for they shall see God"** (Matthew 5:8). The
writer of Hebrews declares **"Follow peace with all men,
and holiness, without which no man shall see the Lord"**

(Hebrews 12:14). The Bible makes it very clear, if we want to see the Lord, we have to have pure, holy hearts.

How do we get a pure heart and clean hands? These deal with both our attitudes (hearts) and our actions (hands). To get clean hands and a pure heart, first we ask God's Spirit to search us. **"Search me, O God, and know my heart; try me, and know my thoughts; and see if there be any wicked way in me, and lead me in the way everlasting"** (Psalm 139:23–24).

Only God can reveal our hearts to us! Jeremiah, the prophet, wrote **"The heart is deceitful above all things, and desperately wicked. Who can know it?"** (17:9). King David tells us that we cannot discern our own errors, and must come to God for acquittal from our hidden secret faults and sins (See Psalm 19:12). The process of getting right with God is letting Him search our hearts for sin, and then we must confess our sin and receive His faithful forgiveness and cleansing.

The church today seems to be using much of her energy,

power, and time attempting to counsel people about areas of their lives which should have been dealt with at conversion. *We must stop allowing the people to blame their past for their present sins*, because the Scriptures teach when you got saved, you lost your past — it is gone! **"Therefore if any man be in Christ, he is a new creature: old things are passed away; behold, all things are become new"** (2 Corinthians 5:17).

Look what happened when Christ came into your life. Ephesians 4:24 says **"Put on the new man which was created according to God, in true righteousness and holiness."** Look at how Paul expresses this in Galatians 2:20 **"I have been crucified with Christ; it is no longer I who live, but Christ lives in me; and the life which I now live in the flesh I live by faith in the Son of God, who loved me and gave Himself for me."**

God's word says "stop trying to bring back to life what He has killed" — your old life. God is saying to this weak bunch of believers "Get over it! Stop going around with the same old problems." It is time for us to bring them to the cross, let Christ deal with them, and go on — go on to maturity. The glory of God is coming to His church in a new strong, tangible measure, and we must die to our old ways and stop clinging to our old excuses to prepare for His glorious presence. The Lord will show us what needs to be removed or rectified if we will ask Him. But it is up to us to let go of old hurts and bitter hearts, and receive the pure hearts Jesus died to give us. After all, the writer in Revelation states **"Be glad, rejoice, for the marriage of the Lamb is come, *and the Bride has made herself ready*"** (19:7, my emphasis).

THE
FATHER'S
HEART
REVEALED

Forgiven - is one of the most liberating and exhilarating words known to mankind. The fact that God is willing, even longing, to forgive fallen man is vital. Pardoned, by God's redemptive love to ponder the thought that by God's mercy and overflowing grace we are being delivered from the bondage of sin's relentless darkness. Releasing all who turn to Christ from the pit of deep despair, releases within us rays of hope. It is completely beyond man's mind to comprehend the awesome grace and mercy of God, whereby God would restore us unto fellowship with Himself. Never forget God is not willing that any should perish but that all should repent and be saved.

The angels that rebelled never knew one single moment

of divine grace offering them restoration and repentance. Yet, God in His tender mercy continues to plead with fallen mankind to turn from sin to eternal salvation. There is no sin so shockingly wicked that it blocks God's mercy and forgiveness. God pleads with a wicked, wayward people **"Come now, let us reason together, though your sins be as scarlet, they can be washed as white as snow; though they are red like crimson, they shall be as wool"** (Isaiah 1:18). The hand of God is extended to all who long for forgiveness and desire to be set free.

On the other hand, neither is sin so trivial that it negates the need for God's extended mercy. Never forget it is the little foxes that spoil the vines (See Song of Songs 2:15). We must not fall prey to the enemy's deception that wants us to believe God is only concerned about the big sin issues in our lives. There is nothing too big or too little to deal with. Now is the time each of us must deal radically with what has separated us from God. God not only wants to remove our glaring flaws, but every small stain upon our heart, for He knows that only those with clean hands and pure hearts will ascend into the presence of the Lord.

God is both the source and substance of our forgiveness. The source of our forgiveness is the heart of God. **"If You, Lord, should mark iniquities, O Lord, who could stand? But there is forgiveness with You, that You may be feared"** (Psalm 130:3–4). The substance that provides the power of our forgiveness is the blood of Christ. The following song, written in the mid-1800s, poses a very powerful question: *"What can wash away my sin?"* Let the powerful words of this song penetrate deep within your soul.

> *What can wash away my sin?*
> > *Nothing but the blood of Jesus;*
>
> *What can make me whole again?*
> > *Nothing but the blood of Jesus;*
>
> *For my pardon this I see,*
> > *Nothing but the blood of Jesus.*
>
> *For my cleansing, this my plea,*
> > *Nothing but the blood of Jesus.*

Nothing can for sin atone,
   Nothing but the blood of Jesus.

Naught of good that I have done,
   Nothing but the blood of Jesus.

This is all my hope and peace,
   Nothing but the blood of Jesus.

This is all my righteousness,
   Nothing but the blood of Jesus.

Oh! Precious is the flow –
   That makes me white as snow.

No other fount I know,
   Nothing but the blood of Jesus.

The Holy Spirit inspired Paul the Apostle to pen these words in Ephesians 1:7 **"In Him we have redemption through His blood, the forgiveness of our trespasses, according to the riches of His grace."** The riches of God's grace have purchased our forgiveness through the precious blood of Jesus, the Lamb of God. Christ, when He instituted communion, reminded us that the forgiveness of our sins is in His blood: **"For this is My blood of the covenant, which is poured out for many for forgiveness of sins"** (Matthew 26:28).

The songwriter, William Cowper, penned these thought-provoking words:

"There is a fountain filled with blood drawn from Emanuel's veins, and sinners plunged beneath its flood lose all their guilt and stain."

Also, I love Elisha Hoffman's song "Are You Washed in the Blood of the Lamb?" *"Have you been to Jesus for His cleansing power, are you washed in the blood of the Lamb"*? Such words seem strange to the ears of a carnal church (and, in fact, much of the unbelieving "church" has been busily removing such songs from their hymnals). The words of another old song "Love Lifted Me" ring in my thoughts: *"I was sinking deep in sin; far from the peaceful shore. Very deeply stained within; sinking to rise no more. But the Master of the sea; heard my despairing cry. From the waters lifted me; now safe am I."* What an awesome God we serve, willing to hear our cries of deep desperation and extend His hand of mercy to pull us from the sea of sin. God will reach deep into the miry clay extending grace and mercy to lift us up and out of this pit of despair and set our feet upon the solid Rock.

The Scripture states that those who have been forgiven much love much. Each of us should pour out our lives in love to the Lord, for we were bound in the bondage of sin deep within a horrible pit. But in His loving-kindness God came and reached down to us, and through forgiveness He lifted us out of the miry clay and freed us from the pit of sin. **"I waited patiently for the Lord; and He inclined to me, and heard my cry. He also brought me up out of a horrible pit, out of the miry clay, and set my feet upon a rock"** (Psalm 40:1–2).

Jesus releases great insights into God's heart on restoration and forgiveness in the parable of the prodigal son found in Luke 15:11–24.

> *And He said, "A man had two sons. The younger of them said to his father, 'Father, give me the share of the*

estate that falls to me.' So he divided his wealth between them. And not many days later, the younger son gathered everything together and went on a journey into a distant country, and there he squandered his estate with loose living. Now when he had spent everything, a severe famine occurred in that country, and he began to be impoverished. So he went and hired himself out to one of the citizens of that country, and he sent him into his fields to feed swine. And he would have gladly filled his stomach with the pods that the swine were eating, and no one was giving anything to him. But when he came to his senses, he said, 'How many of my father's hired men have more than enough bread, but I am dying here with hunger! I will get up and go to my father, and will say to him, "Father, I have sinned against heaven, and in your sight; I am no longer worthy to be called your son; make me as one of your hired men." So he got up and came to his father. But while he was still a long way off, his father saw him and felt compassion for him, and ran and embraced him and kissed him. And the son said to him, 'Father, I have sinned against heaven and in your sight; I am no longer worthy to be called your son.' But the father said to his slaves, 'Quickly bring out the best robe and

> *put it on him, and put a ring on his hand and sandals*
> *on his feet; and bring the fattened calf, kill it, and let*
> *us eat and celebrate; for this son of mine was dead and*
> *has come to life again; he was lost and has been found.'*
> *And they began to celebrate."*

In this passage we discover the high cost of low living. The son set out to spend his inheritance on "high living" only to end up in one of the lowest places. Nevertheless, we see the Father's heart to embrace the broken, repentant son. Once the Lord said to me *"If you would preach repentance like I mean it, you will see more people do it."* The word "repent" can be broken down like this: "re" means *"to put back"* and "pent" means *"the highest place."* Thus, when we repent God picks us up and replaces us to the highest place. This is the revelation of the prodigal son, from the pigpen of sin to the father's loving embrace!

It is crucial that we gain a much clearer comprehension of forgiveness. There are two aspects of forgiveness we need revelation about — God's divine forgiveness for our sins, as well as our need to forgive others their offences against us. Only as we experience both will we be equipped to walk in an upright, victorious life.

The value of the life-altering directive given in Ephesians 4:31–32 is immense **"Let all bitterness, wrath, anger, clamor, and evil speaking be put away from you, with all malice. And be kind to one another, tenderhearted, forgiving one another, even as God in Christ forgave you."**

Notice the motivating factor for forgiveness— we have received the tender mercy of God applied to our life, now we should want to extend mercy to all just as God has to us. You might protest saying "You just don't know what harm they did to me." That is true. However whatever someone has done to us cannot even start to compare to what we have done to Christ. Nevertheless, God in His tender mercy has forgiven us. It is with this same mercy we should forgive one another.

Men and women who do not know forgiveness carry their moral void with them into every area of their daily lives. Unforgiveness fosters bitterness, anger and all types of malice — these are key elements in sickness. Remember, it is a merry heart that does good like a medicine (See Proverbs 17:22). The person that does not know forgiveness is someone void of true peace.

The Prophet Nehemiah reminds us of our stubbornness and God's longsuffering. In Nehemiah 9:17 we discover that God longs to release forgiveness for each of us:

> *They refused to listen and did not remember Your wondrous deeds which You had performed among them; so they became stubborn and appointed a leader to return to their slavery in Egypt. But You are a God of forgiveness, gracious and compassionate, slow to anger and abounding in loving-kindness; and You did not forsake them.*

Notice some of God's attributes listed in this passage:

• God is a God of wondrous, miraculous works.

• God is a God of forgiveness.

• God is a God of grace.

• God is a God of compassion.

• God is a God who is slow to anger.

- God is a God who is overflowing in loving-kindness.
- God is a God who does not forsake.

The prophet's words assist us to better understand that God is a God of love and mercy, longing to release for each of us a much better life than we could ever conceive for ourselves. God longs to release us into a life of victory resulting in a bright future for both now and eternity. Now is the time to cast all our cares completely upon Christ knowing that He is a faithful Friend ready and willing to help us through every issue of life. Open wide your heart and experience the Father's abiding overflowing grace and mercy, He loves you without measure.

Bobby Conner
Eagles View Ministries
www.bobbyconner.org